MW00459854

ILLUMINATING THE DARKNESS

ILLUMINATING THE DARKNESS

Blacks and North Africans in Islam

Habeeb Akande

Ta-Ha Publishers Ltd.

First Published in February 2012
Reprinted 2014

Ta-Ha Publishers Ltd.
Unit 4, The Windsor Centre
Windsor Grove, West Norwood
London, SE27 9NT, UK
www.tahapublishers.com

Written by: Habeeb Akande
Edited by: Abdassamad Clarke

Cover design and Typeset by: N.A. Qaddoura

A catalogue record of this book is available from the British Library

ISBN-13: 978-1-84200-127-1

Front cover image: Ibn Tulun mosque, Egypt

Printed and bound by:
IMAK Ofset, Turkey

Dedicated to my parents

"Lord, show mercy to them as they did in looking after me when I was small."
(Sūrat al-Isrā 17:24)

Transliteration Key

The transliteration convention used throughout this book represents the Arabic script as follows:

أ ا	a,ā	د	d	ض	ḍ	ك	k
ب	b	ذ	dh	ط	ṭ	ل	l
ت	t	ر	r	ظ	ẓ	م	m
ث	th	ز	z	ع	ʻ	ن	n
ج	j	س	s	غ	gh	هـ	h
ح	ḥ	ش	sh	ف	f	و	w,ū,u
خ	kh	ص	ṣ	ق	q	ي	y,ī,i

The definite article is rendered as *al-* before 'moon' letters, thus *al-qamar* remains *al-qamar*, and it is assimilated to the following letter if it is a 'sun' letter, thus *al-shams* is rendered *ash-shams*. The *tāʼ al-marbūṭah* is represented by a final *h*.

Contents

Foreword

This is a timely work. With black people in the US beginning finally to emerge from the centuries of degrading slavery and the false start of the Civil Rights movement, and with Africa itself increasingly looking to be the continent of the future for Islam, nothing written in this area is without politics. Thus, it has been vital for orientalists, themselves often faithful servants of powerful oligarchic elements in world finance and corporatism, to back-project modern racism and the horrific history of Judaeo-Christian slavery into Islam. But make no mistake about it, this is entirely a political issue, or rather we should say an economic one, since today academia serves politics which in turn serves economics.

One should not, in defending against this attack, resort to a rose-tinted and romantic view of the history of the Muslims for, unsurprisingly, Muslims have had their tyrants, murderers, adulterers, drunks and thieves just as have others. And Muslim culture itself has suffered tremendous low-points in its cyclical history, a history which comprises an initial exuberant bursting forth, a high point with its cultural achievements, gradual decline into decadence, followed by renewal, a cycle best exemplified by Madīnah al-Munawwarah itself and often but not exclusively illustrated by the Islam of the West and Africa in particular, of which this book has splendid examples.

The reader needs no other discrimination while reading this book than the one the author strives to make clear throughout: the *dīn* of Islam is not only free of racism but is utterly opposed to it as the most aberrant form of *jāhiliyyah (ignorance)*. This is clear in the Qur'ān, the Sunnah and in the extensive hadith literature.

Where the book is utterly fascinating is in its vignettes of whole African civilisations and 'empires', one uses that term advisedly, that rose and sank, and the fierce resistance mounted against colonialism and its imperial projects, and also of the luminous scholars from an often forgotten tradition that sustained that history. This is a revelation of a kind for those who think of Islamic history exclusively in terms of the great Arab 'empires' of the Middle East and their long decline into decadence and finally extinction. Perhaps few things are more damaging for Muslims' sense of identity today than this spurious identification of Islamic history with that of the Arabs, who are after all, only a small percentage of the Muslims, neglecting in the process the sultanates of the Far East such as in Nusantara (Indonesia and Malaysia), the Mughals of the Indian Sub-Continent, the numerous Turkic Stans that were absorbed into the USSR, the glorious Osmanli dawlah, and the huge and inadequately explored history of Islamic Africa. The book's extensive bibliography contains enough pointers for the reader to pursue that line of enquiry.

Just as the constituency of modern Muslim societies is clear evidence of the absence of racialism and colourism from Muslim hearts at their best, it contains then a sign for the future. Globalisation increasingly mixes peoples up all over the earth and once-subject peoples, impoverished and often made refugees by it, flee to the West. The West's own subject peoples, its indigenous peoples, are also bewildered by the modern age, misled by the media servants of high oligarchic finance. They allow their rage to be deflected from the usurious monetary order of the age onto the flood of the bereft from the once-Third World. It is only Islam that offers a multi-racial brotherhood for the people of the future from both disadvantaged groups. Indeed, it is only Islam that has successfully allowed peoples of different races and religions to live together, as in Andalus and the Osmanli dawlah. When the Muslims themselves wake up from their slumbers and emerge from the ghettoes, both physical and intellectual, that they have foolishly allowed themselves to inhabit, they will have to take their place as generous hosts of humanity in an increasingly alien and predatory age. In having given us resources for that, the author has done us a tremendous service.

Abdassamad Clarke

Introduction

Praise be to Allah Who has honoured the human being and preferred the people of *taqwā* and faith from among them. He made the human heart the area of His concern, not the colours of our skin. He looks at the purity of our intentions and not at our guises or forms. I beseech Him to send His blessings and peace upon the best of creation, the master of the whites and blacks, the leader of the Arabs and non-Arabs, the Chosen One, the Beloved Messenger, the Seal of the Prophets, Muḥammad the son of 'Abdullāh ﷺ.

The message of Islam is the affirmation of the one truth that has always been and will never cease to be – there is no god but Allah. The Arab Prophet of Islam was sent to the whole of humanity. In his final address during the Farewell Ḥajj he proclaimed, "O people! Your Lord is one. Your forefather is one. Truly, there is no superiority for an Arab over a non-Arab, nor is there any superiority for a non-Arab over an Arab, there is no superiority for a black person over a red[1] person nor a red person over a black person, except by *taqwā* (righteousness).

1 See chapter two for an explanation of the colour red, which is often interpreted to refer to whites - Ed.

O people! Bear witness! Have I conveyed [the message]?" They replied in the affirmative. Then the Prophet ﷺ said, "Then let the one who is present today inform the one who is not here."[2]

Unfortunately, after the death of the Prophet ﷺ, some of the Muslims began to deviate from Islam's teachings of racial equality. Among other signs of decadence, Arab ethnocentrism and colour prejudice towards blacks sometimes crept into Muslim thinking and literature as Islam spread across the known world. However, there [illegible] slim writers who attempted to restore the purity of [illegible] producing valuable works citing the virtues and [illegible] ack Africans. Written by a British-born Muslim of African descent, *Illuminating the Darkness* is about blacks and North Africans in Islam. Part I of the book explores the concept of race, 'blackness', slavery, interracial marriage and racism in Islam. Part II of the book consists of a compilation of short biographies of noble black and North African Muslims in Islamic history.

Perception of Blacks

The Arabs' view of blacks in pre-Islamic Arabia is difficult to assess as there is evidence indicating both colour prejudice and racial harmony. Blacks in Arabian history form the subject of a fascinating book by Abduh Badawi entitled *Ash-shu'arā as-sūd wa-khaṣā'isuhum fī ash-shi'r al-'Arabī* ['*The Black Poets and their Characteristics in Arabic Poetry*']. He cites several passages of poetry and 'historical narratives suggesting a strong feeling of antagonism towards and discrimination against blacks in pre-Islamic Arabia. Badawi wrote, "There was a sharp sensitivity over colour among the black poets before Islam. This was because

---

[2] The address, which is from the *khuṭbah* (sermon) during the Farewell Ḥajj, is widely reported throughout the hadith literature. These words are reported from Jābir by Al-Bayhaqī in *Shu'ab al-īmān* 4:289, No. 5137, and from one of those who heard it by Ibn an-Najjār and Abū Nu'aym in *Ḥilyat al-awliyā'* 3:100, No. 5652. Az-Zuḥaylī, 2005, vol. 13, p. 591.

they were a depressed and downtrodden group and because they were excluded, sometimes roughly, sometimes gently, from entering the social fabric of the tribe. Thus they lived on the edge of society as a poor and depressed group."[3] On the other hand, Bernard Lewis in his study of race-relations in Arabia argues the opposite. He cites reports indicating that blacks (particularly Abyssinians) were regarded with respect as people with a level of civilisation substantially higher than that of the Arabs themselves.[4] The Arabs, like every ancient people known to human history, harboured prejudices and hostilities against those whom they regarded as 'other'. However, despite the apparent traces of colour prejudice within pre-Islamic Arabian society, the early Arabs were not racist as racism is understood today. Rather they were tribalistic and viewed tribal affiliation as of the utmost importance, not a person's race or ethnic background.

The advent of Islam in the seventh century of the Christian Era (CE) created a new situation in race relations in the world. Islam, for the first time, gave birth to a truly universal civilisation, extending from Southern Europe to Central Africa, from the Atlantic Ocean to India. Establishing an egalitarian society based on human brotherhood and faith in the One God, Islam was a source of liberation. *Imān* (faith) became the central focus of loyalty and affiliation in the new monotheistic community; "*Indeed the believers are brothers*"[5] Allah proclaimed in the Qur'ān. The Prophet ﷺ called upon the Muslims to be united, regardless of their ethnicity, lineage or social status: "Every Muslim is a brother to a fellow Muslim, neither wronging him nor surrendering

---

3 Badawi, 1973, pp. 223-224.

4 In the sixth century, Abyssinians were active in Arabia as allies of the Byzantines in the great struggle for power and influence between the Christian Roman Empire on the one hand and the Persian Empire on the other. Many Abyssinians remained in Arabia, mostly as slaves, after the Abyssinian king, Abrahah's, unsuccessful attempt to conquer Makkah in the sixth century. Lewis, 1990, p. 25.

5 Sūrat al-Ḥujurāt 49:10.

him to someone else to be wronged. And if anyone helps his brother in need, Allah will help him in his own need."[6] Although hadith literature suggests the continuation of prejudice towards blacks amongst some of the Arabs during the time of the Prophet ﷺ, he ﷺ attempted to eradicate this by severely reprimanding anyone showing any signs of chauvinistic sentiments. The Prophet ﷺ would say, "People should cease boasting about their dead ancestors – they are merely fuel for the Fire – or they will be of less value with Allah than the beetle which moves dung with its nose. Allah has removed from you the pride of *jāhiliyyah* (the pre-Islamic period) and its boasting of ancestors. One is either a believer with *taqwā* or a wretched wrongdoer. All human beings are the children of Adam and Adam was created from dust."[7] On another occasion, the Messenger of Allah ﷺ said, "He is not one of us who calls for *'aṣabiyyah*[8] (tribalism and racism), he is not one of us who fights for *'aṣabiyyah* and he is not one of us who dies for *'aṣabiyyah*."[9] At-Tabrīzī relates in *Mishkāt al-Maṣābiḥ* that Prophet ﷺ said, "If anyone proudly asserts his descent in the manner of the people of ignorance (*jāhiliyyah*) tell him to bite his father's penis, and don't use a euphemism!"[10] Referring to people calling others to support them in

[6] Muslim, *kitāb al-birr wa'ṣ-ṣilah wa'l-adab, bāb taḥrīm aẓ-ẓulm*, No. 2580, and Al-Bukhārī *kitāb al-maẓālim, bāb lā yaẓlimu'l-muslim al-muslim wa lā yuslimuhu*, No. 2310.

[7] At-Tirmidhī, *fī Thaqīf wa Banī Ḥanīfah*, No. 4048, and Abū Dāwūd, *bāb fi't-tafākhur bi'l-aḥsāb*, No. 5116. The wording is that of At-Tirmidhī.

[8] *'Aṣabiyyah* is defined by the Messenger of Allah ﷺ, in a hadith narrated by Al-Bayhaqī in *As-Sunan* from Wāthilah, as, "...that you aid your people in wrongdoing." Where it denotes the natural force of kinship that binds a polity together, it is a key term in the work of Ibn Khaldūn. Many people misunderstand his position. Rather than calling to the forbidden *'aṣabiyyah* in which people support their race or tribe or nation in wrongdoing, Ibn Khaldūn identifies how the natural forces of kinship operate, and moreover, how they work along with the dynamics of the *dīn* in creating Muslim polities, which he illustrates copiously with examples from history - Ed.

[9] Abū Dāwūd, *kitāb al-adab, bāb fi'l-'aṣabiyyah*, No. 5121.

[10] At-Tabrīzī in *Mishkāt al-Maṣābīḥ, kitāb ar-riqāq, bāb al-mufākharah*, second section. He notes that Al-Baghawī narrated it in *Sharḥ as-Sunnah* and he adds, "It is weak."

a conflict on the basis of tribal allegiance, the Messenger of Allah ﷺ said, "Leave it, for it is rotten!"[11] The Prophet ﷺ knew that the social ill of tribalism and racism (*'aṣabiyyah*) would unfortunately remain within some segments of the Muslim community, for he said, "There are four things from the time of ignorance which my community will never give up: boasting about their forefathers' deeds and qualities, casting aspersions on lineage, seeking to be given rain by means of the stars and bewailing the dead."[12] Some of the most prominent figures from the followers of the Prophet ﷺ were of African descent, such as his confidant and *mu'adhdhin*, Bilāl ibn Rabāḥ ؓ. The Qur'ān, the speech of Allah, prohibits the faithful from mocking an individual on any basis whatsoever, particularly something as arbitrary as skin colour, since *"the one being ridiculed may be better than the ridiculer."*[13] Indeed, the Qur'ān acknowledges and speaks about the various colours of mankind, and that they are great signs of the Omnipotent Creator: *"Among His Signs is the creation of the heavens and the earth and the variety of your languages and colours. There are certainly Signs in that for every being."*[14] Racial equality and tolerance in the early Muslim community lasted from the prophetic era through the epoch of the Rightly Guided Caliphs[15] in 661CE.

Towards the end of the seventh century, as the Arab Muslims went forth from the Arabian Peninsula to conquer half of the known world, a sense of Arab superiority began to develop amongst some of the Arab Muslims.[16] Under the Umayyad dynasty, many of the Arabs tended to

superiority complex as a result of empire building

---

[11] Muslim, *kitāb al-birr wa'ṣ-ṣilah wa'l-adab, bāb naṣr al-akh ẓāliman aw maẓlūman*, No. 2584, and Al-Bukhārī, *kitāb al-manāqib, bāb dhikr Qaḥṭān*, No. 3330.

[12] Muslim, *kitāb al-janā'iz, bāb at-tashdīd fī an-niyāḥah*, No. 934; see also At-Tirmidhī and Aḥmad.

[13] Sūrat al-Ḥujurāt 49:11.

[14] Sūrat ar-Rūm 30:22.

[15] Abū Bakr, 'Umar, 'Uthmān and 'Alī ؓ.

[16] As an example of non-Arabs who later came to have a sense of racial superiority, Persians in the Middle Ages perceived their pale brown complexion as the ideal

live separately from the indigenous communities they conquered.[17] Most of their subjects were Christian, Jewish or Zoroastrian, and the Arabs made little effort to convert them.[18] In this period, even to become a Muslim, one had to become a sort of fictive Arab by being adopted as the client (*mawlā*)[19] of an Arab tribe. Non-Arab Muslims were sometimes treated as second-class citizens by some of the Arab aristocracy who were perhaps absorbed with their concern for tribal honour. Subjected to a series of fiscal, social, military, and other disabilities, non-Arab Muslims were known collectively as the *mawālī*, 'clients'.[20] The proud and disdainful behaviour of the Arabs towards the *mawālī*, as it was perceived, did not take long in provoking a reaction amongst the conquered peoples who rose to defend themselves and to declare their equality with the Arabs, using their adopted Arabic

---

between the two extremes of the "murky, malodorous" blacks and the "leprous colouring" of whites. Ibn al-Faqīh, 1885, p. 162, (translated by Bernard Lewis in *Islam, Volume II: Religion and Society,* 1987, p. 209).

17 Initially, the Caliph 'Umar ibn al-Khaṭṭāb ﷺ had ordered the Companions and the Arab tribes to found their own cities, such as Kufa, in the desert rather than living in the conquered Persian cities as he feared them settling down to managing estates and becoming involved in mundane tasks when they had been charged with the spread and establishment of the *dīn* - Ed.

18 This apparent failure to try and convert the non-Muslims is also widely seen as an example of the expansive and tolerant nature of early Muslim society. The conquered nations, such as Egyptians, Syrians and Persians, became Muslims in the subsequent decades entirely without coercion and without pressure - Ed.

19 There were a number of practical reasons for the practice of becoming a *mawlā* of an Arabic tribe or individual, one of which was that the tribe stood by the *mawlā* in the event of his injuring or killing another Muslim if he became due to pay compensation, e.g. a hundred camels in the case of manslaughter, and would help with the payment of that - Ed.

20 One positive aspect of this apparently discriminatory treatment was that large numbers of the *mawālī* rose to positions of great prominence through their acquisition of the sciences of the *dīn*, for all Muslims held people of knowledge in great esteem. Thus, most of the *fuqahā'* (jurists) and *'ulamā'* (scholars) of the generations of the Followers of the Companions were from the *mawālī*, men such as Abū Ḥanīfah, 'Ikrimah, and Nāfi' the freed slave of Ibn 'Umar, et al. This was

language to express themselves, and sometimes adopting heterodox forms of Islam as the symbol of their opposition to Arab domination.[21] This cry for equality had differing reactions in the Muslim world. In the central lands of the Middle East, speakers of languages such as Coptic in Egypt, Syriac and Aramaic in Syria and Palestine, and Chaldean in Iraq, adopted Arabic as their language of learning and of daily speech and, by and large, adopted Arab manners, customs and ways of thinking. Their descendants are the bulk of today's 'Arabs'. Farther east the Persians stuck to their ancient tongue in daily speech and much of their literature and created a distinctly Persian Islamic culture. In the West, the Berbers of North Africa either became Arabised or clung to their indigenous language and culture and were largely marginalised.[22]

The Arab ethnocentrism and colour prejudice which emerged during the Umayyad dynasty created a period of unrest for blacks and Berbers alike. Many blacks were taken as slaves as were Persians and other races in the East, whilst the policies of the Umayyad governors led to the Berber revolt which took place during the reign of Umayyad Caliph Hishām ibn 'Abd al-Malik in 740-743CE. The Berber revolt marked the first successful secession from the Arab caliphate.[23]

Strong feelings were aroused among other non-Arabs, who eventually contributed their support to the Abbasids during their revolution against the Umayyad Caliphate, and they were taken in by Abbasid propaganda that they would reinstitute wise and just governance by

---

further amplified in later generations with huge numbers of the most famous scholars of hadith and other sciences being non-Arabs, such as Al-Bukhārī, At-Tirmidhī and Sibawayh, the grammarian - Ed.

21 This reaction is known as the *shu'ūbiyyah* movement, a movement of mainly Persian Muslims responding to the privileged status of Arabs and the Arabisation of Iran in the ninth century. Two centuries after the *shu'ūbiyyah* movement in the East, the movement re-emerged in Andalusia, i.e. Islamic Spain.

22 Hunwick, 2006, p. 76.

23 Blankinship, 1994, pp. 113-114.

the family of the Prophet ﷺ himself, not aware that it was the more distant relatives through his ﷺ uncle al-'Abbās that were intended. The Abbasid regime took over the Islamic Caliphate in the 750s and after fighting against insurrections led by key members of the family of the Messenger of Allah ﷺ, who were supported by Imams Abū Ḥanīfah and Mālik ibn Anas among others, maintained a relatively unified control of the Muslim world for the next two hundred years from a new capital, Baghdad. However, it was also under their rule that they were forced to acknowledge other centres of power and authority such as that which was to become the Umayyad caliphate of Andalusia and the heretical Fatimid 'caliphate' of North Africa. Nevertheless, it was under the Abbasids that non-Arabs began to be more fully integrated into Muslim society once again. Unfortunately this did not last for long.

In the ninth century, hundreds of black African slaves (*Zanj*) from East Africa were shipped to Iraq to work in salt mines and plantations under the harshest conditions. Humiliated and oppressed, the blacks revolted against the Abbasids in what was one of the greatest rebellions in world history and the first major uprising in the history of the African Diaspora.[24] The *Zanj* rebellion was eventually suppressed and the blacks were once more forced to lead a marginal life. The revolt seemed to have had a huge impact on the perception of blacks in the Muslim world. It was during and after this period that negative stereotypes of blacks began to intensify and proliferate. The Biblical 'curse of Ḥām' story, the Ancient Greeks' natural slave theory

[24] The *Zanj* revolt occurred in the ninth century during the reign of the Abbasid caliph, Al-Mu'tamid. The revolt was fomented by black slaves working in the saline areas of lower Mesopotamia to remove the salt sands and brine and open the area up to cultivation. Some contemporary researchers have said that the revolt was a social conflict and not a racial one as initially thought. Aṭ-Ṭabarī's *Tārīkh ar-rusul wa'l-mulūk* is the primary source for information about the *Zanj* revolt. Aṭ-Ṭabarī, 1987, Volume XXXVII.

and fabricated traditions attributed to the Prophet ﷺ demonising blacks began to appear frequently in Muslim literature. One of these fabricated traditions attributed to the Prophet ﷺ says, "There is no good in Abyssinians, when they are hungry they steal and when satiated they fornicate."[25] Another concocted tradition says to "Beware of the blacks for they are distorted creatures!"[26] Some incautious Arab, Berber and Persian Muslims absorbed these racist statements about blacks and recounted them in their works under the garb of Islam. Negative stereotypes of blacks and others, including indeed 'whites' or *gorras*, have continued in some parts of the Muslim world right up until recent times.

In Defence of Blacks

In response to the negative representations of black people which developed in some Muslim societies in epochs of decline, two approaches emerged. While some writers and poets rose to defend blacks against their detractors in the Muslim community (the resistance model),[27] others accepted the proposed ill-fate of blacks, accepting

---

25 This narration was reported by As-Suyūṭī, Aṭ-Ṭabarānī and Ibn 'Asākir. Al-Bukhārī and Ibn al-Jawzī classified this tradition as fabricated and forged. As-Suyūṭī, 2004, p. 20.

26 The full tradition reads, "Marry like with like and match like with like. Choose carefully your offspring, and beware of the *Zanjī*, for he is a distorted creature." In another forged tradition, the Prophet ﷺ is reported to have said, "Remove the blacks from me. Verily they are black because of their stomachs (i.e. their greed) and private parts (i.e. fornication)." "The *Zanjī*s are donkeys." Ibn al-Jawzī and Al-Bukhārī said that all of the aforementioned traditions are erroneous. Ibn al-Jawzī, 2008, pp. 472–474. Ibn al-Qayyim al-Jawziyyah said that all traditions attributed to the Prophet ﷺ which curse blacks are fabricated. Faisal, 2000, pp. 68-69.

27 Some black poets exploded in the faces of those who alluded to their colour as may be seen in the poetry of the 'three angry poets', Al-Ḥayquṭān, Sunayh and 'Akim of the early eighth century. For them it was not enough just to defend themselves. They took pride in their blackness and black history, attacking the Arabs on matters they prided themselves upon.

the negativity of blackness but asserted the moral and intellectual qualities of blacks (the internalising contempt model).[28] This book is based upon the first approach, the resistance model. *Illuminating the Darkness* presents a variety of influential black and African Muslims in history from black Arabs, to black Africans, to 'white' North African Berbers.[29] In this book I will discuss the concept of race, 'blackness', slavery, interracial marriage and racism within an Islamic framework. This work is by no means the first of its kind; several Muslim writers have dealt with the concept of race and the eminence of blacks in the Islamic literary genre 'the virtues of blacks', which we will now mention very briefly.

Al-Jāḥiz, Ibn al-Jawzī and As-Suyūṭī

Abū 'Uthmān 'Amr ibn Baḥr al-Kinānī al-Jāḥiẓ was a prolific Afro-Arab scholar of East African descent. Born in Iraq, Al-Jāḥiẓ grew in prominence to become one of the greatest Arab satirists and prose writers of his generation. His *Fakhr as-sūdān 'alā al-bīḍān* ['The Boast of the Blacks over the Whites'] is regarded as the earliest work from the 'virtues of blacks' Islamic literary genre.[30] Al-Jāḥiẓ lived during an era marked by a visible increase in overt racial hostility from Arabs

---

[28] Al-Baqir al-Afif Mukhtar in his article 'The Crisis of Identity in Northern Sudan: A Dilemma of a Black People with a White Culture' points out that with such manifest (colour) prejudices, two kinds of reactions occurred in the Muslim world: resistance and internalising contempt. However resistance itself took two approaches: one challenged the stereotypical image and declared that 'black is beautiful' and the other accepted the prevailing prejudice that it is ugly, apologised for it and celebrated the human and moral qualities of blacks. Mukhtar, p. 35.

[29] The Berbers are the indigenous peoples of North Africa whose skin colour varies from white to dark brown.

[30] The literary genre about the blacks is not dissimilar to the Islamic literary genres of the virtues of the Arabs, Persians and Turks. See Taqī ad-Dīn ibn Taymiyyah, *Manāqib ash-Shām wa ahlihi*, Abū al-Ḥasan ar-Rabī', *Faḍā'il ash-Shām wa Dimashq* and Abū Bashīr al-Ḥajūrī, *Al-Qawl al-ḥasan fī faḍā'il ahl al-Yaman.*

against black Africans. One of the most extreme reactions to this was the massive slave insurrection in the late ninth century, the *Zanj* Rebellion. In the treatise, Al-Jāḥiẓ discusses the global history of blacks and explores the concept of 'blackness' in Arab culture. In the essay Al-Jāḥiẓ assigns traditional Arab virtues and praiseworthy qualities to blacks such as generosity, courtesy and oratory. Al-Jāḥiẓ attributes these qualities, as well as physical strength, the art of dancing and cheerfulness to blacks. The treatise has four main sections: a register of famous blacks in history, the argument for black superiority, positive aspects of the colour black and the noble qualities of black people.[31] Abū al-'Abbās 'Alī ibn Muḥammad al-Anbarī wrote a similar treatise entitled *Risālah fī faḍl as-sūdān 'alā al-biḍān* ['An Epistle about the Superiority of Blacks over Whites']. A third work, *Kitāb as-sūdān wa faḍluhum 'alā al-bīḍān* ['Blacks and their Superiority over Whites'] was written by Abū Bakr Muḥammad ibn Khalaf al-Baghdadī ibn al-Marzubān.[32] A fourth book, *Kitāb manāqib as-sūdān* ['Merits of Blacks'] was written by Abū Muḥammad Ja'far ibn Aḥmad ibn as-Sirāj al-Qārī. Khalīfah ibn Abī al-Faraj az-Zamzamī al-Makkī ash-Shāfi'ī wrote *Kitāb rawnaq al-ḥisān fī faḍā'il al-ḥubshān* ['The Book of the Beautiful Water Concerning the Virtues of Abyssinians']. All of the aforementioned books apart from Al-Jāḥiẓ's treatise are lost.

At the beginning of the thirteenth century, Abū al-Faraj 'Abd ar-Raḥmān ibn al-Jawzī, the celebrated traditionalist from Baghdad, produced his valuable addition to the 'virtues of blacks' genre, *Tanwīr al-ghabash fī faḍl as-sūdān wa'l-ḥabash* ['Illuminating the Darkness

---

31 Although some commentators have interpreted Al-Jāḥiẓ's treatise as a parody of the Persian *shu'ūbiyyah* movement, Al-Jāḥiẓ appears, behind the satirical façade, to be genuinely concerned with the plight of blacks within Muslim society. To this end, he dwells on their compliance with traditional Arab virtues and how favourably blacks measure up to Islamic ethical standards. Colville, 2002, p. 25.

32 Both this work and the preceding one were probably written during or just before the *Zanj* revolt in Baghdad. Alawiye, 1985, p. 37.

Concerning the Virtues of Blacks and Abyssinians']. Ibn al-Jawzī was a prolific writer, powerful orator and hadith master. *Tanwīr* is a pietistic historical summary of the social history of black Africa and the meritorious deeds of some well-known persons of African descent in the eastern Islamic world. In *Tanwīr*, Ibn al-Jawzī attempts to raise the morale of blacks and remind them of the status of some noble black personalities in history.[33] Written in a narrative style with twenty-eight chapters of unequal length, *Tanwīr* covers most of the topics Al-Jāḥiẓ addresses in *Fakhr as-sūdān 'alā al-bīḍān*. However, for all its importance, *Tanwīr* has been criticised for its lack of originality and creativity; like many of Ibn al-Jawzī's works, *Tanwīr* is a monographic compilation made up of traditions and poems written by Ibn al-Jawzī's predecessors. Ibn al-Jawzī is reported to have said, "I am an editor, not a writer."[34] Ibn al-Jawzī's work is largely derived from written sources, but oral sources are also cited. Although not a pioneer in the field, Ibn al-Jawzī's book had a far-reaching influence on those who came after him, none more so than the acclaimed Arab polyhistor, Jalāl ad-Dīn as-Suyūṭī. As-Suyūṭī, a teacher of some of the greatest scholars to emerge from West Africa, was interested in the situation of Africans (particularly Abyssinians). He wrote a few books in honour of Abyssinians, enumerating their praiseworthy qualities and elevated status in Islam. His first book *Raf' sha'n al-Ḥubshān* ['Raising the Status of Abyssinians'] is, according to As-Suyūṭī, "a more complete and abridged version" of Ibn al-Jawzī's *Tanwīr al-ghabash*. As-Suyūṭī's other work *Azhār al-'urūsh fī akhbār al-Ḥubūsh* ['Flowers of the Thrones Concerning Reports about Abyssinians'] is an abridgement of his first book in the genre, *Raf' sha'n al-Ḥubshān*.

---

33 Ibn al-Jawzī says, "I saw a group of eminent Abyssinians who were disheartened because of their colour. I explained to them that respect is granted in accordance with good deeds rather than by a pleasant appearance, thus I wrote this book to recall the virtues of a great many of the Abyssinians and blacks." Ibn al-Jawzī, 1998, p. 29.

34 Muḥammad, 1985, p. 52.

A third book by As-Suyūṭī entitled *Nuzhat al-'umr fī at-tafḍīl bayna al-bīḍ wa as-sūd wa as-sumr* ['The Promenade of a Lifetime Concerning Preference for Light-Skinned, Dark-Skinned and Brown-Skinned People'] is an anthology of verse in praise and satire of differently coloured women. After As-Suyūṭī, Muslim authors began to imitate Ibn al-Jawzī's and As-Suyūṭī's works in their books of the virtues of blacks and Abyssinians, works such as: *Aṭ-ṭirāz al-manqūsh fī maḥāsin al-Ḥubūsh* ['The Coloured Brocade Concerning the Good Qualities of Abyssinians'] by Muḥammad ibn 'Abd al-Bāqī al-Bakhārī, *Mir'āt al-Ḥubūsh fī al-uṣūl* ['The Reflection of the Abyssinians in the Sources'] by 'Alī ibn Muṣṭafā, *A'lām at-ṭirāz al-manqūsh* ['Notification of The Coloured Brocade'] by 'Alī ibn Ibrāhīm al-Ḥalabī ash-Shāfi'ī and *Kitāb al-jawāhir al-ḥisān bimā jā'a 'an Allāh wa ar-Rasūl wa 'ulama at-tārīkh fī al-Ḥubshān* ['The Book of Exquisite Jewels from what has come from Allah, the Messenger and the Historians regarding Abyssinians'] by Muḥammad al-Hifnī al-Qana'ī all are important works in this field, but none of these works produced anything original nor achieved the fame of Ibn al-Jawzī's or As-Suyūṭī's works. The very existence of the vast number of books in defence of blacks is a reflection of the prejudice blacks were subjected to in medieval Muslim society.

Since the composition of As-Suyūṭī's book more than half a millennium ago, I felt obliged to include some eminent African personalities of Islam who have lived during the long period since. In order to refine the compilation, I have also included North African (Berbers) and West African Muslims in addition to the East African (Abyssinian) and Central African (Sudanese) Muslims cited in the aforementioned scholars' works.[35] *Illuminating the Darkness* is an opportunity for the English reader to read about the Islamic literary genre on the virtues of blacks and North Africans in Islam. Recent times have witnessed

---

35 Ibn al-Jawzī's *Tanwīr* focuses on two ethnic groups of Africa: the Sudanese and Abyssinians, whilst As-Suyūṭī's works are dedicated to the Abyssinians.

the emergence of a wave of contemporary scholars critically addressing the issue of racism and colourism within the Muslim community and classical Muslim literature. However a thorough examination of the institutionalised racism within contemporary Muslim societies will not be addressed in this book as it would require an in-depth sociological study, which is beyond the scope of this work.[36]

The Structure of the Book

Following in the tradition of the famous literati who have preceded me in this topic, I have structured this book according to a similar monographic arrangement. The book consists of fifteen chapters in two parts. All prophetic traditions are referenced and I have relied on the acumen and scholarship of classical hadith specialists for the verification of prophetic traditions.[37]

In the first chapter I will examine the representation of the colour black and 'blackness' in classical Arabic and the two textual sources of Islam, the Qur'ān and hadith. The next chapter, chapter two, deals with the constructions of race and ethnicity according to the vernacular of the early Arabs. The origins of the peoples of Africa are discussed in chapter three from an Islamic anthropological perspective. Chapter four critically examines Muslim scholars' differing aetiologies regarding the 'cause' of black peoples' skin colour. Chapter five delves into the controversial topic of the enslavement of black Africans by Arab and North African Muslims and the validity of slavery in the modern era. Chapter six is an exposition of some of the wisdoms and benefits

---

[36] Bernard Lewis's book *Race and Slavery in the Middle East* is an interesting historical and anthropological study of the development of race relations in Muslim societies.

[37] The classifications of hadith masters such as As-Suyūṭī, Ibn Ḥajar, Adh-Dhahabī, Al-Ḥākim, Ibn al-Jawzī and Al-Bukhārī have been taken into account for the verification of prophetic traditions related in this book.

of brown and dark skin. An enumeration of the praiseworthy qualities of blacks, Berbers and Copts from the works of traditional Muslim scholars like Al-Jāḥiẓ, Ibn al-Jawzī and Ibn Baṭṭūṭah is presented in chapter seven. The following chapter, chapter eight, discusses the topic of interracial marriage in Islam. The honoured status of black Africa is presented in chapter nine. Gathered from the works of Muslim traditionalists, the compilation of notable black and North African Muslims forms the second part of the book. Chapter ten begins with the black prophets, while black male and female Companions of the Prophet ﷺ are listed in chapters eleven and twelve respectively, African religious scholars in chapter thirteen, African Muslim rulers and kings in chapter fourteen and in the final chapter fifteen, African warriors and martyrs. The book is concluded with a summary of the superiority of *taqwā* in Islam.

I hope that this book will enlighten its readers as to the ennobled status of blacks and North Africans in Islam. Perhaps this book can help to erase some of the unfortunate misconceptions about blackness and those of African descent that have been in many cases exacerbated by racist thinking. The figures mentioned in this work were all inspired by the Islamic faith which was the catalyst for their triumphs and success. Superiority and true virtue in Islam reside in *taqwā* (consciousness of and obedience to Allah) alone. I ask Allah the Exalted to make me and the reader amongst His right-acting slaves.

PART I

1

The Arabic Language and the Colour Black

The Qur'ān was revealed in the Arabic tongue, the Messenger of Allah ﷺ was an Arab and the initial custodians of the prophetic message were predominately Arabs. Therefore, the relationship of the Arabic language with the religion of Islam is inseparable; Arabic is an integral part of the divine revelation, thus an examination of the early Arabs' use of their language is paramount in order to acquire an accurate interpretation of the Qur'ān. Traditional scholars of Islam such as Imam ash-Shāfi'ī[1] and Ibn Taymiyyah[2] went as far as saying that studying the Arabic language is a religious obligation upon every Muslim. The prominent Andalusian legal theoretician and grammarian, Abū Isḥāq ash-Shāṭibī stresses, in his famous book *Al-Muwāfaqāt,* the importance of comprehending the multiple connotations and meanings of Arabic words rather than just the apparent and literal senses.[3] He argued that a lack of familiarity with classical Arabic along

1 "It is obligatory upon every Muslim to learn the Arab tongue to the utmost of his power in order (to be able) to profess through it that 'There is no god but Allah and Muḥammad is His slave and Messenger' and to utter in mentioning what is incumbent upon him." Khadduri, 2008, p. 93.

2 Ibn Taymiyyah, 2003, pp. 188-189.

3 Ash-Shāṭibī, 2006, pp. 306-325.

with its linguistic nuances and ancillary sciences would seriously hamper one's understanding of Islam and its two sources, the Qur'ān and the Sunnah. That being the case, I will commence the book with an examination of the multiple meanings of the word 'black' and its usage in classical Arabic and Islamic sources.

Etymology

According to Arabic lexical sources, *aswad* (black) is literally the opposite of white. *Aswad* is derived from the root *s-w-d*; it has many associated meanings, such as: *sawād* (literally 'blackness'), meaning a group of palm trees, the settled areas around a village or town, the great majority of people (*as-sawād al-a'ẓam*), and great wealth. The two staples of the desert Arabs' diet, dates and water, are referred to as 'the two black things' (*al-aswadān*). The word *sayyid* is from the same root as black or blackness, *s-w-d*. Depending on the context, it means: lord, master, honourable, virtuous, generous, forbearing or leader. For a person to be literally called 'more black' (*aswad*)[4] than someone else would mean he is more majestic.[5]

Islam and its Attitude Towards the Colour Black

The idea that black is connected with sin, evil, deviltry and damnation, while white has the opposite associations, is common in many languages. However in the Arabic language and early Arab culture there were many positive connotations and associations connected with the colour black (*aswad*). The colour black and its associations are used in Islam and classical Arab culture in both a laudatory and a pejorative

---

4 "'*Aswad*': *Greater,* and *greatest, in respect of estimation, rank,* or *dignity;* synonymous with '*Ajall*' [more majestic]: (S, K:) and, as some say, *more* [and *most*] *liberal* or *bountiful* or *munificent:* or more [and *most*] *clement* or *forbearing. ...* Also *Black.*" Lane's *Arabic-English Lexicon* - Ed.

5 Ibn Manẓūr, 2003, vol. 4, p. 737; Al-Fayrūzābādī, 2009, pp. 771–772; Ar-Rāzī, 2005, p. 289 and Shakir, p. 4.

context. Black has no special status distinguishing it from other colours, nor is it considered evil or hideous as it is in other religious traditions. The Arabs referred to themselves as 'black' in comparison to the 'red' Persians.[6] *Aswad* and *Sawdā*, literally meaning 'black' in the masculine and feminine forms respectively, were popular names amongst the Arabs. The root *s-w-d* denoting black or blackness occurs ten times in the Qur'ān; three times it has the meaning of lordship (*as-siyādah*),[7] blackness (*as-sawād*) occurs five times figuratively as a description of a condition[8] whilst the other two uses of the word black are used to describe the mountains and the night.[9]

Whilst some have argued that the Arabic language and the religion of Islam are prejudiced against black people and 'despise' the colour black, a study of the Arabic language and Islamic sources proves that this allegation is false. An example of a Qur'ānic verse used as 'evidence' of anti-black sentiment in Islam is, "*On the Day when faces are whitened and faces are blackened. As for those whose faces are blackened: 'What! Did you disbelieve after having believed? Taste the punishment for your disbelief!' As for those whose faces are whitened, they are in Allah's mercy, remaining in it timelessly, for ever.*[10] The Orientalist Bernard Lewis says the following, "It is obvious that no reference to black and white races is intended in this passage, which makes use of the common Arabic idiom shared with many languages, even including those of black Africa – associating whiteness with joy and goodness, blackness with suffering and evil." The 'blackening of the faces' refers to punishment and not to skin colour, 'Abd al-Qādir Kāmil says in

---

6 Ibn Manẓūr, 2003, vol. 4, p. 738.

7 The word (*sayyid*) occurs in the context of praise, censure and the third instance in an expository passage without praise or blame. Sūrah Āl 'Imrān 3:39, Sūrah Yūsuf 12:25 and Sūrat al-Aḥzāb 33:67.

8 The word 'black' appears twice in Sūrah Āl 'Imrān 3:106. The same word is used in Sūrat az-Zumar 39:60, Sūrat an-Naḥl 16:58 and Sūrat az-Zukhruf 43:17.

9 Sūrat al-Baqarah 2:187 and Sūrah Fāṭir 35:27-28.

10 Sūrah Āl 'Imrān 3:106-107.

his excellent study of race and Islam entitled, 'Islam and the Race Question'.[11] Commenting on the aforementioned verses, Zaid Shakir, an American Muslim scholar says, "Many Qur'ānic exegetes mention that this does not refer to physical whitening for the righteous, nor physical blackening for the sinners. The great exegete, (Abū as-Su'ūd) al-'Imādī, mentions that the whitening and blackening of the face are allegories for, respectively, the manifestation of great happiness or dejection on the Day of Rising. That being the case, even though the 'whitening' of the face is identified with a positive referent, great happiness, it is not associated with any racial or ethnic grouping in this world, nor does it have any actual association with a physical colour. Therefore it cannot be viewed as a term that prejudices any human group. In fact, the Prophet Muḥammad ﷺ is related as mentioning that on that day in the life hereafter, the faces of black people will be the 'whitest' (i.e. most illuminated).[12] If one were to interpret the Qur'ān in a literal fashion, which is necessary to see it prejudicing a particular group, then the negativity associated with the term 'black' and hence its prejudicing black people would be offset by other (Qur'ānic) verses, such as, *'On the day when the trumpet will be blown, We will gather the wrongdoers with blue eyes (zarqā).'*[13] Were one to interpret this verse literally, as I (Zaid Shakir) have translated it, one could say that it clearly prejudices Northern Europeans, the people most commonly found with blue eyes."[14] Classical Qur'ānic exegetes clearly dismiss such an interpretation, pointing out that the word *zarqā* carries various meanings. Ibn 'Abbās said that the blue eyes refer to blindness, for eyes that have been afflicted with cataracts take on a bluish colour and lose their capacity for sight. Aṭ-Ṭabarī said that the look of the wrongdoers' eyes will be blue out of the intense

---

[11] Kāmil, 1970, p. 49.
[12] Ibn al-Jawzī, 1998, pp. 145–147.
[13] Sūrah Ṭā-Hā 20:102.
[14] Shakir, p. 4.

thirst they will experience at the time of the assembly. Al-Bayḍawī said, "The sinners are described as having blue eyes because blue was considered the worst and most detestable eye colour to the Arabs. The Romans who were the Arabs' greatest and most loathsome enemies had blue eyes."[15] Ibn Kathīr said the eyes will be blue as a result of the fright they will experience. As we can see from the aforementioned comments, the blue eyes (*zarqā*) mentioned in the verse are allegorical and are void of any worldly racial or ethnic associations.

Trajectio Ad Absurdum

Arabic literature and poetry is full of figurative expressions, metaphorical imagery and rhetorical devices. Since the Qur'ān was revealed in the Arabic language, Allah naturally makes use of the conventional linguistic devices of the Arabs in conveying His message. One rhetorical device common in classical Arabic usage is 'an argument by the absurd', *trajectio ad absurdum,*[16] a device very different from *reductio ad absurdum*. The purpose of the *reductio ad absurdum* is to demonstrate the falsity of an argument by stating it in its most extreme and therefore most absurd form. The Arabic rhetorical device has the opposite purpose, i.e. not to disprove but to emphasise and reaffirm. In *trajectio ad absurdum,* a proposition is asserted and a highly unlikely, even absurd, example is given. The purpose is to show that the principle still applies even in this extremely unlikely and absurd formulation. The colour black is often used to point out this type of argument in Arabic and Islamic literature. For example, the Prophet ﷺ used this rhetorical device when he wanted to stress the importance of obedience to the legitimate Islamic authority, however unlikely the form in which it appears: "Listen and obey, even if an Abyssinian is given authority over you, whose head is

15 Al-Bayḍawī, 2001, p. 654.
16 Term coined by Bernard Lewis.

as if it was a raisin."[17] Another example is the prophetic tradition, "Do not marry women for their beauty for perhaps their beauty may ruin them, and do not marry them for their wealth for perhaps their wealth may make them disobedient, but instead marry them for their *dīn*. A black slave woman with a perforated nose who has the *dīn* is better."[18] These examples are not 'racist' as some modern readers might think, rather they illustrate the importance of, on the one hand, being dutiful to the established order and, on the other, that *dīn* is more important than the incidental qualities of a woman, i.e. her physical beauty and wealth. One must also understand the mind-sets of the people being addressed in these statements, i.e. the Arabs. The Arabs before the advent of Islam were an unlettered, simple people who lacked the sophistication of the Romans and Persians. The Arabs' contact with blacks was minimal and the blacks they did come into contact with were mainly slaves, thus it would have been difficult for them to envisage a black slave as a political leader. Likewise a black slave-girl with a facial disfigurement would have been difficult for them to envisage as a bride, particularly considering the fact that they preferred fair-skinned women. What is emphasised here is submission to the established order and looking for *dīn* in a marital partner, not that there is something inherently wrong with black skin.

The Messenger of Allah ﷺ also used the *trajectio ad absurdum* device to emphasise the importance of establishing justice in political affairs. During his lifetime, a woman of the Banū Makhzūm (a noble Arab clan) stole and was due to be punished. Some of the men of

---

17 Al-Bukhārī, *kitāb al-jamā'ah wa'l-imāmah, bāb imāmat al-'abd wa'l-mawlā*, 661, 664.

18 Ibn Mājah, vol. 1, p. 597, No. 1859; Al-Bayhaqī 7:80, No. 13247; 'Abd ibn Ḥamīd, p. 133, No. 328; Al-Bazzār, 6:413, No. 2438. All cite from As-Suyūṭī *Jam' al-Jawāmi'*. Very weak hadith. Al-Būṣīrī said one of the narrators in this *isnād*, Al-Ifrīqī (full name 'Abd ar-Raḥmān ibn Ziyād ibn An'am ash-Sha'bānī) is weak.

Quraysh thought it intolerable that judgement should be executed upon a woman of Makhzūm and deliberated about who would be able to speak to the Prophet ﷺ and convey the people's intercession to him. They decided upon Usāmah ibn Zayd, who was beloved to the Prophet ﷺ. The Messenger of Allah ﷺ rejected Usāmah's mediation, and rebuked him, "Usāmah! Would you dare intercede in the matter of one of the legal limits ordained by Allah?" He then stood up and addressed the people, "Those that came before you were only destroyed because it was their practice that if a noble man stole, they would let him go unpunished, but if a weak man stole they would implement the legal punishment upon him. By Allah! Even if Fāṭimah, the daughter of Muḥammad stole, I would cut off her hand!"[19] The Prophet ﷺ did not intend by this statement to insinuate that his daughter might steal, rather the 'even if' phrase was said in order to emphasise the justice of the Prophet ﷺ in implementing the ruling of Allah for anyone who broke His law, even if the perpetrator was a member of his family.

Distinguished Things which are Black in Islamic Culture

Zaid Shakir explores Islam's view of black and blackness in his article, '*Islam, Prophet Muḥammad and Blackness*'. Shakir argues, "One of the reasons Islam proved a source of positive signification (among blacks) is found in its positive view of blackness and black people."[20] Examining Islamic and Arabic lexical sources, Muslim scholars such as Ibn al-Jawzī cite many positive associations and symbols related to the colour black in Islam:

---

[19] Al-Bukhārī narrated it in his *Ṣaḥīḥ* in *Kitāb al-ḥudūd, bāb iqāmati'l-ḥudūd 'alā ash-sharīf*, 8:199; Muslim in his *Ṣaḥīḥ* in *Kitāb al-ḥudūd, bāb qaṭ' as-sāriq ash-sharīf wa ghayrihim*, No. 1688; At-Tirmidhī, *abwāb al-ḥudūd, bāb mā jā'a fī kirāhiyyah an yushfa'a fī al-ḥudūd*, No. 1430, and At-Tirmidhī said, "It is a *ḥasan ṣaḥīḥ* hadith." An-Nasā'ī, Abū Dāwūd and Ibn Mājah also narrated it.

[20] Shakir, p. 2.

1. The *Kiswah* – The black cloth covering the Ka'bah.[21]
2. *Al-Ḥajar al-Aswad* (The Black Stone) – The only object Muslims kiss in reverence as an act of worship.[22]
3. *Al-Ḥabbat as-Sawdā'* (Black Seed)[23] – The Prophet ﷺ said, "This Black Seed is a cure for every type of ailment except for death (*as-sām*)."[24]
4. The black standard – The Messenger of Allah ﷺ used a black standard for his military expeditions as did the Abbasid dynasty.[25]
5. Kohl (*kuḥl*) – "The best eye make-up is antimony (*kuḥl*),"[26] says Al-Jāḥiẓ. Ibn al-Qayyim adds, "*Ithmid* is the best type of kohl used for the eye."[27]
6. Black fruits – Talking of the fruit of the *Arāk* tree, the Prophet ﷺ is reported to have said, "You should take the black ones of them for they are the sweetest."[28]

---

21 The Ka'bah is now always draped in black. This practice dates back to the beginning of the Abbasid Caliphate. However, before that, it was known to have been draped in cloths of various colours. Shakir, p. 4.

22 Sālim narrated that his father ['Abdullāh ibn 'Umar] said, "I saw the Messenger of Allah when arriving in Makkah, and when he saluted the Black Stone at the beginning of performing *ṭawāf*, hastening in three of the seven circuits." Al-Bukhārī, *kitāb al-ḥajj, bāb istilām al-ḥajar al-aswad ḥīn yaqdumu Makkata awwala mā yaṭūfu wa yamūlu thalāthan*, No. 1526.

23 Nigella Sativa, black cumin seeds, also known as *shūnīz.*

24 Al-Bukhārī, *kitāb aṭ-ṭibb, bāb al-ḥabbat as-sawdā'*, No. 5363, and Muslim, *kitāb al-alfāẓ min al-adab wa ghayrihā, bāb at-tadāwī bi'l-ḥabbat as-sawdā'*, No. 2215. At-Tirmidhī, Aḥmad, Aṭ-Ṭabarānī, Ibn Mājah and Ibn Ḥibbān, and others also narrate the same hadith or others with similar wordings and meanings. As-Suyūṭī says, "Black seed is useful in counteracting all diseases that are cold and wet. It is also used in treating hot diseases when combined with other remedies, in order to accelerate their penetration. The uses of black seed are many." As-Suyūṭī, 1994, p. 50-51. Ibn al-Qayyim al-Jawziyyah says, "Black seed is beneficial for all cold illnesses." Ibn Qayyim al-Jawziyyah, 2008, p. 215.

25 Ibn Majah, No. 2818.

26 Al-Jāḥiẓ, 2000, vol. 1, p. 146.

27 Ibn Qayyim al-Jawziyyah, 2003, p. 251.

28 Al-Bukhārī, *kitāb al-anbiyā', bāb ya'kufūna 'alā aṣnāmin lahum*, No. 3225.

2

Race and Skin Colour

The racialised discourse prevalent in modern times was alien to pre-Islamic Arabs and early Muslims. Black Africans were not considered to be genetically different to 'black Arabs', as Al-Jāḥiẓ elucidates in his treatise, *Fakhr as-sūdān 'alā al-bīḍān*.[1] A report from Al-Bukhārī indicates this: when a fair-skinned Arab Bedouin's wife bore a black child, he suspected that she might have been guilty of infidelity, so he went to the Messenger of Allah ﷺ to seek his counsel. The Prophet ﷺ informed the Bedouin that his child probably inherited his dark complexion from one of his forefathers. The Bedouin did not object to the rationale, as it was common to have 'black Arabs'.[2] The majority of 'pure' Arabs are said to have been brown in complexion, though there

---

1 Al-Jāḥiẓ says, "Our blackness, O people of the *Zanj*, is not different from the blackness of the Banū Sulaym and other Arab tribes." Al-Jāḥiẓ, 2000, vol. 1, p. 148.

2 Al-Bukhārī relates: A Bedouin came to the Messenger of Allah ﷺ and said, "Messenger of Allah, my wife has given birth to a black child." He ﷺ said to him, "Have you got camels?" He said, "Yes." He ﷺ asked, "What colours are they?" He said, "They are red." He ﷺ asked, "Are any of them grey?" He said, "Yes." He ﷺ asked, "How could that have happened?" He said, "I think it was a hereditary disposition that he resembled." He ﷺ said, "Perhaps your child inherited his colour from his ancestors." Al-Bukhārī, *kitāb al-muḥāribīn min ahl al-kufr wa'r-riddah, bāb mā jā'a fī at-ta'rīḍ*, No. 6455, see also No. 4999.

are many Arabs with varying skin tones ranging from very fair to very dark. Although Arabic literature suggests some incidents of colour prejudice in pre-Islamic Arabian society, it was not a racist society as racism is understood in the modern context.[3] The Arabs did not have a racial typology to divide people from different ethnic groups into specific races. The Arabs' descriptions of people's complexions were relative and descriptive and terms such as 'white' and 'black' were not used to suggest a racial connotation as they are today. Bernard Lewis, one of the few contemporary scholars to examine the concept of race and colour in Arab history and Islam, says, "Human beings are frequently described (by Arabs) by words which we might translate as black, white, red, olive, yellow and two shades of brown, one lighter and one darker. These terms are usually used in a personal rather than an ethnic sense and would correspond to such words as 'swarthy', 'sallow', 'blonde' or 'ruddy' in our own modern usage more than to words like 'black' and 'white'. Sometimes they are used ethnically but even then in a relative rather than absolute sense. The Arabs, for example, sometimes describe themselves as black in contrast to Persians, who are red, but at other times as red or white in contrast to the Africans, who are black."[4] There are many terms that describe human complexions in classical Arabic that have different meanings from contemporary usages of the same terms. We will look at some of these terms and how they were used by the early Arabs.

3 Bernard Lewis did not find any anti-black sentiment in his analysis of race relations in pre-Islamic Arabian society. It was not until the seventh century conquest of Africa and the enslavement of some of its inhabitants that colour prejudice began to surface in Muslim society. "The ancient Middle Eastern peoples harboured all kinds of prejudices and hostilities against those whom they regarded as 'other'. But the 'other' was primarily someone who spoke another language (the prototypal barbarian) or professed another religion (the Gentile or Heathen)." Lewis, 1990, p. 17.

4 Lewis, 1990, p. 22.

Abyaḍ (White)

The Arabs' use of the word 'white' was relative and was mainly used for fair-skinned peoples. The Romans (Europeans) and Persians were considered 'white' in comparison to the Arabs, whilst the Arabs were 'white' in contrast to the black Africans. 'White' could also be used metaphorically for dark-skinned peoples. Tariq Berry points out in his book *The Unknown Arabs*, "The term white can be very confusing to those reading about the description of people of the past because, in the past, when Arabs described someone as white, they meant something entirely different from what is meant today. In the past, when the Arabs described someone as white, they meant either that he had a pure, noble essence or that he had a nice, smooth complexion without any blemishes. They meant he had a black complexion with a light-brownish undertone."[5] Ibn Manẓūr, the acclaimed Arab linguist of the thirteenth century says in his Arabic lexicography, *Lisān al-'Arab*, "When the Arabs say a person is *abyaḍ* (white), they mean that he has a pure, clean, faultless character, they do not necessarily mean that he has white skin. So when the Arabs say, 'So-and-so has a white face', they mean that he is free from blemishes and defects." The ninth century linguist Ath-Tha'labī informs us, "The Arabs do not say that a man is white because of a white complexion; 'white' to the Arabs means that a person is pure, without any faults."[6] Thus a person described as 'white' by the early Arabs may have been pale-skinned or had a brownish complexion. Unfortunately some pseudo-Islamic cults of recent times have put forward the theory that when the Arabs used the word 'white' they were actually referring to blacks, thus when the Prophet Muḥammad ﷺ was described as white in authentic prophetic traditions, it means he was actually black! This type of reasoning is

---

5 Berry, 2001, p. 49.

6 Ibn Manẓūr, 2003, vol. 1, pp. 563-568.

absurd and unheard of from traditional scholars of Islam.[7] Traditional scholars of Islam are in agreement that the Prophet ﷺ was most certainly not black or African as pseudo-Islamic groups propagate in modern times.[8]

Aḥmar (Red)

Aḥmar (red) was a term used by the Arabs to describe what we would today call 'white people'; the term was generally used to refer to the Byzantine Romans and Persians of that time. Ibn Manẓūr says that the expression 'the red people (*al-Aḥmar*)' applies to the non-Arabs (Byzantine Romans and Persians) because of the paleness of their skin. Adh-Dhahabī says, "Red, according to the vernacular of the people of the *Ḥijāz*, means fair-skinned and this complexion is rare amongst the Arabs." Thus when the Prophet ﷺ said, "I was sent to the *aḥmar* (red) and *aswad* (black people)"[9], Ibn Manẓūr says, "By the 'red' people the Prophet ﷺ means the non-Arabs, and by the 'black' he means the Arabs. This is because the majority of the Arabs are brown in complexion, whereas the majority of non-Arabs (i.e. Romans and Persians) are of a pale and ruddy complexion." Ath-Tha'labī was asked, "Why do the Arabs specifically use *aḥmar* (red) and not *abyaḍ* (white) when referring to white people?" He replied, "This is because *abyaḍ* (white) to them was someone pure without any defects. They would not call someone who is *abyaḍ* (white) in complexion, *abyaḍ* (white). Rather they would say he is *aḥmar* (red)."[10]

---

7 Qāḍī 'Iyāḍ reports: Aḥmad ibn Abū Sulaymān, the companion of Saḥnūn said, "Anyone who says that the Prophet ﷺ was black should be killed." 'Iyāḍ, 2006, p. 375.

8 Pseudo-Islamic black sects of recent times include: the Nation of Islam, the Five Percenters and the Moorish Science Temple of America.

9 Muslim and Aḥmad.

10 Ibn Manẓūr, 2003, vol. 2, p. 586.

Aswad (Black)

When the Arabs of the past used the word *aswad* (black) to describe a person, they usually meant that the person's complexion was actually very dark. *Aswad* was used descriptively rather than in an ethnic sense. The Arabs would say '*aswad*' (black) or '*shadīd al-udmah*' (extremely dark) to describe any person of a dark complexion. Ibn Manẓūr reports, "Pure blooded Arabs described themselves as 'black', whilst non-Arabs were described as 'red'."[11] Al-Jāḥiẓ says regarding the Arabs' perception of 'black skin' in *Fakhr as-sūdān 'ala al-bīḍān*, "The Arabs take pride in black skin! This might seem surprising given that their compliments typically include epithets like 'fair', 'bright', 'spotless' and 'lily-white'. However, it is not the whiteness of a man's skin to which these refer but his integrity."[12] Blacks were referred to as *Aswad*, *Ḥabashī* (Abyssinian) or *Zanj* in early Arab literature. The early Arabs were not aware of the various tribal and ethnic groups amongst the Africans, so the generic term, *sūdān* (plural of *aswad*) was used to refer to all blacks. Sub-Saharan Africa was called *Bilād as-Sūdān*, literally 'the land of the blacks'. Yet, only a few centuries after the advent of Islam, the word *'abd* (slave) was used to refer solely to blacks. *Ibn as-Sawdā'* (literally, the son of a black woman)[13] and *gharab* (crow) were derogatory terms used by the Arabs to refer to blacks.

---

11 Ibn Manẓūr, 2003, vol. 5, p. 123.

12 Al-Jāḥiẓ uses 'black' to describe all people of colour in *Fakhr as-sūdān 'alā al-bīḍān*, "The *Zanj*, Abyssinians, Fazzānis, Berbers, Copts, Nubians, Zaghāwis, Marwis, Sindis, Indians, Comorans, Daibulis, Chinese and Indo-Chinese are all black!" Al-Jāḥiẓ, 2000, vol. 1, p. 148.

13 This is seriously deprecated because of a specific instance in the *sīrah*:

Al-Ma'rūr said, "I met Abū Dharr at ar-Rabdhah wearing a set of clothing [consisting of a wrap for the lower body (*izār*) and a wrap for the upper body (*ridā'*)] and his slave also wearing a set of clothing, and so I asked him about that. He said, 'I abused a man and found fault with his mother [by calling him "son of a black woman (*ibn as-Sawdā'*)"] and the Prophet ﷺ said to me, "Abū Dharr, you have found fault with his mother, you are a man who yet has some ignorance in him. [They are] your brothers and your uncles whom Allah has put under your power.

Aṣfar (Yellow)

The fair-skinned Byzantine Romans (Europeans) were referred to by the Arabs as *Banū Aṣfar*, literally 'the yellow people', i.e. the fair-skinned people. Ibn al-Athīr said that the Romans were called *Banū Aṣfar* because their ancestor was of a (pale) yellow complexion.[14] The terms 'black' and 'yellow' were used interchangeably at times. In *Kitāb al-Aghānī* ['The Book of Songs'] by Abū al-Faraj al-Aṣbahānī, Sa'īd ibn Misjah, the famous black Arab singer of the ninth century, is described as yellow. Ibn Manẓūr says, "Yellow can also mean black."[15]

Akhḍar (Green)

The word *akhḍar* (green) is used synonymously with the colour 'brown or dark-skinned' when describing peoples' complexion.[16]

Udmah (Dark-skinned)

Ibn Manẓūr says concerning the term *ādam,* a derivative of the word *udmah,* "When (the term *ādam* is) used to describe an individual's complexion, it means very dark-skinned. It is said that the term comes from the expression the 'face' or 'surface of the earth' which means the colour of the earth. From this word, Adam, the father of mankind, received his name." The prophet Adam عليه السلام was also said to have received the name Adam due to his dark skin complexion.[17]

Whoever has his brother under his power should feed him from what he eats himself and dress him from what he wears himself. Do not impose on them what will overcome them, and if you impose something on them, then help them."'" Al-Bukhārī, *kitāb al-īmān, bāb al-ma'āṣī min amr al-jāhiliyyah, wa lā yukaffaru ṣāḥibuhā bi'rtikābihā illā bi'sh-shirk,* No. 30, see also Nos. 2407 and 5703.

14 Ibn Manẓūr, 2003, vol. 5, p. 352.

15 Ibn Manẓūr, 2003, vol. 5, p. 348.

16 Ibn Manẓūr says that *al-akhḍar* means *aswad al-jildah*, 'dark-skinned' when referring to peoples' complexion. Ibn Manẓūr, 2003, vol. 3, p. 122.

17 Ibn Manẓūr, 2003, vol. 13, p. 105.

Asmar (Tawny Brown)

The colour *asmar* (tawny brown) was used by the Arabs to refer to someone with a fair or brown complexion. Ibn Manẓūr says that the Prophet ﷺ was described as being *asmar* (i.e. fair in complexion) and in another narration the Messenger of Allah ﷺ is described as being very fair (literally white, *abyaḍ*) with a reddish tone.[18] Ibn Manẓūr said the majority of Arabs are brown (*sumrah*) in complexion.[19]

---

18 Ibn Manẓūr, 2003, vol. 4, p. 675.

19 Ibn Manẓūr, 2003, vol. 2, p. 586.

3

Anthropology

In traditional Muslim thought, Ḥām is regarded as the progenitor of all the black Africans with whom there is associated the 'curse of Ḥām' story. Ibn Khaldūn, the acclaimed polymath, rejected the 'silly story' of Ḥām being the ancestor of Africans saying, "Genealogists who had no knowledge of the true nature of things imagined that blacks were the children of Ḥām (Ham), the son of Nūḥ (Noah)."[1] Some of the reports and traditions stating that Ḥām is the forefather of all Africans are weak and belong to the *Isrā'īliyyāt*[2] category of Islamic traditions. Muslims, as per the instruction of the Messenger of Allah ﷺ, are obliged to refrain from either affirming such reports or totally

---

[1] Ibn Khaldūn, (translated by Franz Rosenthal), 2005, p. 59.

[2] The *Isrā'īliyyāt* are narratives from Judaeo-Christian sources. There are some prophetic traditions that permit the narration of *Isrā'īliyyāt*. Al-Bukhārī narrates on the authority of 'Abdullāh ibn 'Amr that the Prophet ﷺ said, "Convey from me, even if it is one *āyah*. Narrate from the Children of Israel without fear of reproach. And whoever lies about me deliberately should prepare his seat in the Fire." (Al-Bukhārī, *kitāb al-anbiyā', bāb mā dhukira 'an Banī Isrā'īl*, No. 3274). In another narration, Abū Hurayrah ؓ said, "The People of the Book used to read the Tawrāh in *'Ibrāniyyah* (Hebrew) and explain it in Arabic to the people of Islam (i.e. the Muslims), so the Messenger of Allah ﷺ said, 'Do not believe the People of the Book, nor disbelieve them, but rather *"Say, 'We believe in Allah and what has been revealed to us...'"* (Sūrat al-Baqarah 2:135).'" (Al-Bukhārī, *kitāb at-tafsīr, bāb qūlū āmannā billāhi wa mā unzila ilaynā*, No. 4215, see also Nos. 6928 and 7103).

disregarding them, as their authenticity cannot be ascertained.[3] Despite this, many classical Muslim writers adopted and propounded the doctrine that blacks were descendants of the 'cursed' son of Nūḥ ﷺ, Ḥām. We will narrate what has been transmitted by Muslim traditionalists and historians regarding Ḥām.

At-Tirmidhī reports in his compilation of prophetic traditions on the authority of Samurah that the Messenger of Allah ﷺ said, "Nūḥ had three sons: Sām, Ḥām and Yāfith. Sām is the ancestral father of the Arabs, Ḥām is the ancestral father of the Abyssinians[4] and Yāfith (Japheth) is the ancestral father of the Greeks (ar-Rūm)."[5] As-Suyūṭī narrates on the authority of Ibn 'Abbās ﷺ that he said, "There were born to Nūḥ: Sām, and amongst his children are white and brown peoples, and Ḥām, whose descendants are blacks with some whites, and Yāfith, whose descendants are fair-skinned and ruddy peoples, and Kan'ān, and he was the one who drowned, and the Arabs call

---

[3] The *Isrā'īliyyāt* narrations are divided into three categories:

1. Those narrations which are confirmed by the Qur'ān or Sunnah and such narrations may be accepted since the Qur'ān confirms their authenticity;
2. Those narrations which contradict the Qur'ān, Sunnah or Islamic teachings, for example, the Bible ascribes evil deeds to certain prophets, such as Nūḥ ﷺ becoming drunk, Lūṭ's ﷺ incestuous relations with his daughters and Dāwūd ﷺ conspiring at the death of one of his generals so that he could marry his wife. These types of narrations are clearly false and should not be believed. The prophets are infallible and are protected from committing major wrong actions;
3. Those narrations concerning which the Muslims have no knowledge. The majority of *Isrā'īliyyāt* narrations fall under this category; it is permissible to narrate such narrations, but these reports are neither affirmed since they might be false nor outrightly rejected as they might be true. Qadhi, 1999, pp. 317-320; Von Denffer, 2007, pp. 133-134.

[4] This *ṣaḥīḥ* hadith does not say that Ḥām was the forefather of all Africans and of all black people but of the Abyssinians - Ed.

[5] At-Tirmidhī, *abwāb tafsīr al-Qur'ān 'an Rasūlillāh ṣalla'llāhu 'alayhi wa sallam, sūrah wa'ṣ-Ṣāffāt*, Nos. 3283-4; see also No. 4023. As-Suyūṭī, 2004, p. 13. The first part is also narrated by Al-Ḥākim, No. 4006 and Aḥmad narrated three versions all from Samurah.

him Yām."[6] Aṭ-Ṭabarī reports that Sa'īd ibn al-Musayyīb said, "Nūḥ begat three, each one of whom begat three: Sām, Ḥām and Yāfith. Sām begat the Arabs, Persians, and Greeks, in all of whom there is good. Yāfith begat the Turks, Slavs, and Ya'jūj and Ma'jūj, in none of whom there is good. Ḥām begat the Copts, the Blacks, and the Berbers."[7] Aṭ-Ṭabarī narrates in another narration: "Among the descendants of Ḥām, the son of Nūḥ, are the Nubians, the Abyssinians, the Fezzanites, the Indians, the Sindhis and the peoples of the coastlands in the East and the West."[8] Ibn Qutaybah narrates in *Kitāb al-ma'ārif,* that Wahb ibn Munabbih said, "Ḥām, the son of Nūḥ, was a white man, with a handsome face and a fine figure, and Allah changed his colour and the colour of his descendants in response to his father's curse. He went away, followed by his sons, and they settled on the shore, where Allah increased and multiplied them. They are the blacks (*as-sūdān*). Their food was fish, and they sharpened their teeth like needles, as the fish stuck to them. Some of his children went to the West Maghrib. Ḥām begat Cush (Kūsh), Canaan (Kan'ān) and Fūṭ. Fūt settled in India and Sindh[9] and their inhabitants are his descendants. Cush and Canaan's descendants are the various ethnicities of blacks: Nubians,[10] *Zanj*,[11] Qarān,[12] Zaghawa,[13] Abyssinians,[14] Copts,[15] and Berbers."[16] Al-Kisā'ī

6 As-Suyūṭī, 2004, p. 14. At-Ṭabarī, *Tārīkh aṭ-Ṭabarī*, 2008, vol. 1, p. 118.

7 Aṭ-Ṭabarī, (translated by William M. Brinner), 1987, vol. II, p. 21.

8 Aṭ-Ṭabarī, (translated by William M. Brinner), 1987, vol. II, p. 15.

9 A province of present-day Pakistan.

10 Nubians are an ethnic group originally from Northern Sudan and Southern Egypt.

11 The *Zanj* are an East African ethnic group or Bantu speaking peoples. *Zanj* was a name used by medieval Arab geographers and genealogists to refer to both a certain portion of the East African coast and its inhabitants.

12 The Qarān or Goran are an African tribe from present-day Chad.

13 The Zaghawa are an ethnic tribe from Eastern Chad and Western Sudan.

14 The Ethiopian Empire was known as Abyssinia. The Ethiopian Empire consisted of Ethiopia, Eritrea, Djibouti and Northern Somalia.

15 The Copts are an ethnic group of Ancient Egypt.

16 Ibn Qutaybah, 1969, p. 26, (translated by Bernard Lewis in *Islam, Volume II: Religion and Society,* 1987, p. 210).

narrates a similar tradition in *Qiṣaṣ al-Anbiyā* ['Tales of the Prophets'].[17] Ibn al-Jawzī reports, "Cush, Niras, Maw'a and Bawān are descendants of Ḥām. Nimrod was a descendant of Cush. This Nimrod was the first of the Mesopotamian monarchs. He ruled three hundred years after the Flood (of Nūḥ's people). During Nimrod's reign the earth divided and people dispersed in the land; from there the different lineages of families were formed. The Nimrod of the Prophet Ibrāhīm was from the descendants of the first Nimrod. From the offspring of Niras were the Turks and Persians. From the loins of Maw'a came Ya'jūj and Ma'jūj. The Slavs, Nubians, Abyssinians, Indians and Sindhis are descendants of Bawān. When the offspring of Nūḥ dispersed in the earth, some of Ḥām's descendants settled on the Southern river-banks, others on the Western river-banks. Allah made them various colours; most of them were dark complexioned but there were also some fair-skinned inhabitants. They are the majority of the inhabitants of the earth."[18]

---

17 Ka'b al-Aḥbār said: "When Nūḥ died, Ḥām lay with his wife, and Allah opened his gall-vesicle and that of his wife also, so that they mingled and she conceived a black boy and girl. Ḥām despised them and said to his wife, 'They are not mine!' 'They are yours!' said his wife, 'For the curse of your father (referring to Nūḥ's supplication against Ḥām, see Chapter 4) is upon us.' After that he did not approach her until the children had grown, when he again lay with her, and she bore two more black children, male and female. Ḥām knew that they were his, therefore he left his wife and fled. When the first two children grew up, they went out in search of their father; but when they reached a village by the edge of the sea, they stayed there. Allah sent desire to the boy so that he lay with his sister, and she conceived. They remained in that village with no food except the fish they caught and ate. Then she gave birth to her brother's children, a black boy and girl. Ḥām, meanwhile, returned seeking the two children and, not finding them, died soon afterwards of anxiety over them. His wife also died, and the other two children set out in search of their brother and sister until they came to a village by the shore, where they stayed. Then they joined the other two along with their own two children. They remained there and each brother lay with his sister, begetting black male and female children until they multiplied and spread along the shore. Among them are the Nubians, the Blacks, the Berbers, the Sindhis, the Indians and all the blacks: they are the children of Ḥām." Al-Kisā'ī, (translated by Wheeler M. Thackston Jr.), 1997, pp. 107-108.

18 Ibn al-Jawzī, 1998, p. 34.

4

Aetiology

If Islamic theology and jurisprudence are colour-blind, history suggests that many Muslim writers were most certainly not. There is a considerable body of ethnographic literature written by Arab and Persian Muslims in the Middle Ages. One of the most controversial issues of debate was the 'cause' and 'reason' behind the darkness of black peoples' skin. Muslim hegemonies over large areas of the world, and their subsequent encounters with people of different colours and physiognomies naturally generated ethnographic literature and aetiologies of the new population groups. There were three recurring aetiologies cited in classical Islamic literature: the curse of Ḥām, environmental determinism and the type of mud from which Adam عليه السلام was created.

1. The Curse of Ḥām

Several Muslim writers report a divine curse aetiological theory. The Curse of Ḥām, also called the Curse of Canaan[1] refers to a story in the

---

[1] Some traditions state that the object of Nūḥ's عليه السلام curse is Canaan, whilst in other reports Ḥām is the object of the 'curse'. This contradiction is an indication of the unreliability of such reports.

book of Genesis 9:18-25, in which Ḥām's father, Nūḥ ﷺ, places a curse upon Ḥām's son, Canaan, after Ḥām saw the nakedness of his drunken father.[2] Transmitted to Muslims by Jews and Christians, the Curse of Ḥām story found its way into early Muslim historiography and ethnography. In contrast to the story found in the Bible, the Muslim versions of the story state that Ḥām's descendants will be cursed with black skin. The curse of Ḥām fable is cited by many medieval Muslim writers and Qur'ānic exegetes as the cause of the darkness of black peoples' skin. Early Muslim scholars such as Ath-Tha'labī,[3] Al-Kisā'ī,[4] Ibn Kathīr and Ibn Qutaybah all narrate the story in their works. Ibn Jarīr aṭ-Ṭabarī reported the fable in his magisterial work on Islamic history, *Tārīkh ar-rusul wa'l-mulūk* ['The History of the Prophets and Kings'], "The people of the Tawrāh claim that this curse was because of Nūḥ's invocation against his son Ḥām. This was because while Nūḥ slept his genitals were exposed, and Ḥām saw them but did not cover

---

2 We have already seen that the story contains an unacceptable error and fatal flaw, the alleged drunkenness of Nūḥ ﷺ, which is impossible for a prophet - Ed.

3 Ath-Tha'labī narrates that Qatādah said: "There were in the Ark only Nūḥ, his wife and three sons: Sām, Ḥām, and Yāfith, and their wives – all in all eight persons. Ḥām had intercourse with his wife in the Ark, and Nūḥ prayed to his Lord," Qatādah said, "and Ḥām's sperm became altered and he brought forth black (offspring)." Ath-Tha'labī, (translated by William M. Brinner), 2002, p. 97.

4 Al-Kisā'ī reports: It is said that one day Nūḥ came to his son and said, "My son, I have not slept since I boarded the Ark, and now I desire to sleep to my fill." So saying, he put his head on Sām's lap and went to sleep. Suddenly a gust of wind uncovered Nūḥ's genitals; Ḥām laughed, but Sām jumped up and covered him. When Nūḥ awoke he asked, "What was the laughter?" Sām told him what had happened, and Nūḥ grew angry with Ḥām. "Do you laugh at your father's genitals?" he said. "May Allah change your complexion and may your face turn black!" And that very instant his face did turn black. Turning to Sām, he said, "You covered your father: may Allah shield you from harm in this world and have mercy on you in the next! May He make prophets and nobles of your progeny! May He make bondswomen and slaves of Ḥām's progeny until the Day of Rising! May He make tyrants, kings and emperors of Yāfith's progeny!" Al-Kisā'ī, (translated by Wheeler M. Thackston Jr.), 1997, p. 105.

them and the two of them (i.e. Sām and Yāfith) threw a garment over him and concealed his genitals. When Nūḥ awoke from his sleep he knew what Ḥām had done as well as what Sām and Yāfith had done. He said, 'Cursed is Canaan the son of Ḥām. Slaves will they be to his brothers!' Then he said, 'May Allah my Lord bless Sām, and may Ḥām be a slave of his brothers. May Allah requite Yāfith and let him alight at the dwelling places of Sām, and may Ḥām be a slave to them.'"[5] Ibn al-Jawzī, the great Muslim traditionalist, said the story is erroneous, "As for what has been narrated that Nūḥ's nakedness was exposed and no one admonished him so he became dark in complexion. This is something not proven and is not correct! There is no evidence which indicates such an event took place, it is quite clear that human complexions are a creation of Allah. There is no clear evidence from sacred sources which suggest otherwise!"[6] As-Suyūṭī says, "The Curse of Ḥām story is a fabrication!" Al-Jāḥiẓ and Ibn Khaldūn[7] as well as contemporary Jewish and Christian scholars state that the Curse of Ḥām story is a myth.[8]

2. Environmental Determinism Theory

The second aetiology for the darkness in human complexions is the environmental determinism theory. Despite stating that the colours of mankind occur by the decree of Allah, Ibn al-Jawzī seems to adopt

---

5 Aṭ-Ṭabarī, (translated by William M. Brinner), 1987, vol. II, pp. 11-12; As-Suyūṭī, 2004, p. 116.

6 Ibn al-Jawzī, 1998, p. 35.

7 Ibn Khaldūn says, "Genealogists who had no knowledge of the true nature of things imagined that blacks were the children of Ḥām, the son of Nūḥ, and that they were singled out to be black as a result of Nūḥ's curse, which produced Ḥām's colour and the slavery God inflicted upon his descendants. It is mentioned in the Torah [Gen. 9:25] that Nūḥ cursed his son Ḥām. However, no reference is made in the curse to blackness." Ibn Khaldūn, (translated by Franz Rosenthal), 2005, p. 59.

8 See David M. Goldenberg's 2003, *The Curse of Ham: Race and Slavery in Early Judaism, Christianity and Islam.*

the environmental determinism aetiology.[9] He says in *Tanwīr al-ghabash*, "There is a report which has been narrated from some of our scholars that the children of Nūḥ dispersed in the lands after Nūḥ's death. It is said that Qāligh ibn 'Ābir was the one who divided them in the lands. Amongst them were the blacks as well as the whites. The children of Sām settled in the centre of the land. They were a mixture of brown and white complexioned people. The children of Yāfith are said to have settled on the Northern and Eastern river-banks. They were of a reddish complexion. The descendants of Ḥām settled on the Southern and Western river-banks. It is said that it was here that their complexion changed (i.e. became darker due to the climate)."[10] Another adherent of environmental determinism was the great Arab prose writer Al-Jāḥiẓ who explained how the environment can determine the physical characteristics of the inhabitants of a certain community. He used his theory of natural selection to explain the origins of different human skin colours, particularly black skin, which he believed to be the result of the climate. He cited a stony region of black basalt in the Northern Najd as evidence for his theory.[11] Ibn Khaldūn, perhaps the most original medieval Arab writer, sought to refute the genealogical arguments for blackness of skin that originate in the Hamitic myth and to replace them with a climate-based theory. In *Al-Muqaddimah*, Ibn Khaldūn attempts to 'scientifically' explain how black peoples' dark skin occurred due to the hot climate of sub-Saharan Africa and not due to Nūḥ's curse.[12] Shams ad-Dīn

---

9 There is no contradiction between the two since the Decree of Allah works through the mechanisms of causality - Ed.

10 Ibn al-Jawzī, 1998, p. 35.

11 Al-Jāḥiẓ, 2000, vol. 1, p. 158.

12 "The black skin common to the inhabitants of the first and second zones is the result of the composition of the air in which they live, and which comes about under the influence of the greatly increased heat in the south. People there go through a very severe summer, and their skins turn black because of the excessive heat." Ibn Khaldūn, (translated by Franz Rosenthal), 2005, pp. 59-60.

Muḥammad ibn Abū Ṭālib ad-Dimashqī, a fourteenth century Syrian writer, is another proponent of climatic factors being the cause of the darkness of skin. Drawing copiously upon earlier writers and popular perceptions, Ad-Dimashqī adds little original argument to the debate. His work unfortunately echoes some prejudices against black people that were not uncommon in his time.[13]

3. The Colour of the Mud from which Adam عليه السلام was Created

The Qur'ān mentions that Adam عليه السلام was created from *"sounding clay of altered black smooth mud."*[14] There are varying opinions amongst Muslim scholars regarding Adam's عليه السلام residence on Earth; some say India whilst others say somewhere in sub-Saharan Africa.[15] Recent studies by leading anthropologist Cheikh Anta Diop, have shown that the first inhabitants of Earth were black and from East Africa.[16] Linguists and lexicographers are also in some disagreement with regards to the origin of Adam's عليه السلام name. Arabic lexicographers state that the word *ādam* is not of Arab origin, and others say that the word Adam is derived from the word *adamah* meaning 'earth'. Ibn Manẓūr says, "There is some disagreement concerning the origin of the name of Adam. Some people say that he was named Adam because he was created from the skin (*adamah*) of the earth. Other people say that he was named Adam because of the *udmah* (tawny) complexion that

---

[13] "The equatorial region is inhabited by communities of blacks who are to be numbered among the savages and beasts. Their complexions and hair are burnt and they are physically and morally deviant." Ad-Dimashqī continues, "Their blackness is due to the sun since its heat is extreme." Ad-Dimashqī, 1923, pp. 15-17 and p. 273, (translated by John Hunwick in *West Africa, Islam and the Arab World*, 2006, pp. 81-82).

[14] Sūrat al-Hijr 15:26.

[15] Ath-Tha'labī, (translated by William M. Brinner), 2002, p. 53.

[16] Cheikh Anta Diop, the late African anthropologist said, "We are able today to say scientifically with certainty that mankind was born in Africa on the latitude of Kenya, Ethiopia and Tanzania." See Cheikh Anta Diop, 1991, *Civilisation or Barbarism: An Authentic Anthropology* and Cheikh Anta Diop, 1974, *The African Origin of Civilisation: Myth or Reality*.

Allah created in him." Ibn Manẓūr continues, "The lexicographers say: the origin of our father Adam's name is from the fact that he was created from soil and similarly, the tawny colour resembles the colour of soil."[17] Although Adam ﷺ was reported to have been dark in complexion, the variation of human colours resulted from the type of mud from which Adam was created. As-Suyūṭī quotes an authentic tradition from the Prophet ﷺ to support this opinion. As-Suyūṭī says, "The Curse of Ḥām story is erroneous! A narration I received on the authority of Umm al-Faḍl[18] supports this: Abū Mūsā al-Ash'arī ﷺ reported that the Prophet ﷺ said, 'Allah created Adam from a handful of the earth. The children of Adam were brought forth according to the type of earth from which they were created. Some are of a reddish complexion, some fair and others black and in between. Some are easy natured and some rough, and some are foul whilst others are good.'"[19] As-Suyūṭī goes on to say, "This hadith is authentic and is an authoritative proof as an explanation for the various colours of mankind. The matter is one which goes back to the type of mud from which Adam was created." This aetiological theory is also held by Ibn Kathīr and Aḥmad Bābā.[20]

---

17 Ibn Manẓūr, 2003, vol. 1, pp. 104-105.

18 All of the narrations are through Ibn Zuhayr not Umm al-Faḍl.

19 At-Tirmidhī, *abwāb tafsīr al-Qur'ān 'an Rasūlillāhi ṣalla'llāhu 'alayhi wa sallama, wa min sūrat al-Baqarah,* No. 4031, At-Tirmidhī said that the hadith is *ḥasan ṣaḥīḥ*; Abū Dāwūd, *kitāb as-Sunnah, bāb fi'l-qadar,* No. 4683; Ibn Ḥibbān, vol. 14, *kitāb at-tārīkh, bāb bad' al-khalq, dhikr al-bayān bi'anna qawlahu ṣalla'llāhu 'alayhi wa sallama, khalaqa'llāhu Ādama min adīmi al-arḍi kullihā, arāda bihi min qabḍatin wāḥidatin minhu,* No. 6160, and As-Suyūṭī, 2004, p. 115.

20 Bābā at-Tinbuktī, (translated by John Hunwick and Fatima Harrak in *Mi'rāj aṣ-ṣu'ūd*, 2000, pp. 30-31).

5

Islam and Slavery

Despite the historical fact that the Arab-Muslim enslavement of black Africans and others pre-dates and post-dates the Western-Christian slave trade, very little has been written by academics and thinkers alike regarding the forced migration of black Africans into the Mediterranean world of Islam and the broader question of slavery within Muslim societies.[1] Islam, like Judaism and Christianity, acknowledges the existence of slavery, but Islam exhorts the faithful to treat slaves kindly and denounces any form of cruelty to slaves. In early Islam, under the instruction of the Prophet ﷺ, slaves were not only treated as the brothers of free men, the Qur'ān told the faithful that a slave who believes in Allah and His Messenger ﷺ is better than a noble free-born pagan.[2] *not critical enough*

As early as the ninth century, hundreds of black Africans were shipped to Iraq to work as slaves. In the eyes of many medieval Arab, *slavery is still ownership of another human being*

---

[1] Hunwick and Powell, 2007, p. xi; Azumah, 2001, pp. 14-18.

[2] *"Do not marry women of the idolators until they believe. A slave-girl who believes is better for you than a woman of the idolators, even though she may attract you. And do not marry men of the idolators until they believe. A slave who believes is better for you than a man of the idolators, even though he may attract you."* Sūrat al-Baqarah 2:221.

Berber and Persian Muslims, blacks were legitimate slaves because they were not People of the Book but were pagans.[3] According to Ibn Sina (d. 1038) blacks are "people who are by their very nature slaves."[4] Blacks were viewed as inherently inferior, destined by God to be enslaved for the service of others. Ibn Khaldūn (d. 1406), the highly acclaimed sociologist, also concurred with this doctrine saying, "The blacks as a rule are submissive to slavery, because they have attributes which are quite similar to dumb animals."[5] During the reign of the Umayyads, the Arabic word *'abd* (a slave) went through a semantic development and came to specifically refer to a black slave, whilst a white slave was referred to as *mamlūk*. By the seventeenth century, *'abd* in spoken Arabic, contrary to the Qur'ān and the Sunnah, very often meant a black person, irrespective of the person being a slave or not.[6]

In David M. Goldenberg's ground-breaking study of the representation of black Africans in Judaism, Christianity and Islam, he says, "The Biblical story (Curse of Ḥām) has been the single greatest justification for black slavery for more than a thousand years. It is a strange justification indeed, for there is no reference in it to blacks at all."[7] The Bible's 'curse' of servitude (not blackness) fell on the youngest son of Ḥām, Canaan, and not his other sons, including Cush (who was later projected in Judaeo-Christian traditions as the ancestor of blacks). The Biblical Curse of Ḥām story in Genesis 9:18-25 follows:

---

3 An important difference between 'pagans', e.g. animists, and other conquered peoples is that People of the Book are offered to live in a *dhimmah* contract with the Muslims under Muslim governance, but that is not possible with people who are not of the People of the Book. Many other peoples came under this same rule, so that Turks and Circassians etc., who were not Christians or Jews, would not have been offered the choice of living under Muslim governance but would have been enslaved by the conquering forces if they did not accept Islam - Ed.

4 Azumah, 2001, p. 135.

5 Ibn Khaldūn, (translated by Franz Rozenthal), 2005, p. 59.

6 Azumah, 2001, pp. 128-130.

7 Goldenberg, 2003, p. 1.

> The sons of Noah who went forth from the Ark were Shem, Ham, and Yapheth. Ham was the father of Canaan. These three were the sons of Noah; and from these the whole earth was peopled. Noah was the first tiller of the soil. He planted a vineyard; and he drank of the wine, and became drunk, and lay uncovered in his tent. And Ham, the father of Canaan, saw the nakedness of his father, and told his two brothers outside. Then Shem and Yapheth took a garment, laid it upon both their shoulders, and walked backwards and covered the nakedness of their father; their faces were turned away, and they did not see their father's nakedness. When Noah awoke from his wine and knew what his youngest son had done to him, he said, "Cursed be Canaan; a slave of slaves shall he be to his brothers."[8]

In contrast to the Biblical account, many Muslim versions of the story portray Arabs as descendants of Sām, blacks (sometimes including the Copts, Berbers and the Sindh of India) as descendants of Ḥām whilst most assigned the Turks and Slavs as descendants of Yāfith. In some Muslim accounts, blacks are condemned to slavery and menial labour, the Arabs are blessed with prophethood and nobility and the Turks and Slavs are destined to be rulers and tyrants.[9] Some narrations of the story of Nūḥ عليه السلام and his sons were attributed to the Prophet ﷺ to give the story a sense of authenticity, but the scholars of hadith filtered out such narrations and classified them as fabricated. The Hamitic myth continued to have currency in the Middle East as late as the seventeenth century during the reign of the Ottoman Empire. During this period many blacks continued to be subjugated to lives of slavery and some of the men were castrated,[10] based on

---

8 Genesis 9:18-25, RSV.

9 Aṭ-Ṭabarī, (translated by William M. Brinner), 1987, vol. II, pp. 10-17.

10 Castration of a human being is *ḥarām* - Ed.

the assumption that they had an ungovernable sexual appetite. The women sometimes did not fare much better, many of them lived a life of domestic servitude or served the sexual appetites of their Arab and Turkish slave masters, as concubines.[11] Aḥmad Bābā (d. 1627), a prominent West African jurist set out to dislodge the notion that black skin was inexorably connected to the condition of servitude in his legal treatise on the enslavement of black Africans, *Miʿrāj aṣ-ṣuʿūd ilā nayl ḥukm majlūb as-sūd* ['The Ladder of Ascent Towards Grasping the Law Concerning Transported Blacks'].[12] Bābā insisted that the cause of slavery in Islam is the content of one's belief and not the colour of one's skin. "The Sudanese (black) non-believers are like other *kāfir* (non-believers) whether they are Christians, Jews, Persians, Berbers, or any others who stick to non-belief and do not embrace Islam. There is no difference between all the *kāfir* in this respect. Whoever is captured in a condition of non-belief, it is legal to own him, whoever he may be, but not he who was converted to Islam voluntarily, from the beginning."[13] Aḥmad Bābā went on to cite other renowned Muslim scholars such as As-Suyūṭī to support the view that slavery in Islam is premised along creedal rather than racial lines. Bābā refuted arguments formed from the myth of Ḥām.

---

11 Slavery is a complex issue and many slaves, men and women, came to exert considerable influence and even power - Ed.

12 In 1615, Aḥmad Bābā replied to questions from Ibrāhīm al-Jirārī, an inquirer from the Saharan oasis of Tuwāt. Bābā says, "You asked: 'What is the meaning of Ḥām's children being slaves to the children of Yāfith and Sām? If he meant the unbelievers, then this is not a peculiarity of theirs (i.e. not all unbelievers are black). On the contrary, it is so in regard to the children of his brothers Yāfith and Sām, since unbelief allows their being possessed (as slaves), whether they are black or white.' The reply is that the legal position is like that. This is not a peculiarity of theirs. Indeed, any unbeliever among the children of Ḥām or anyone else may be possessed (as a slave) if he remains attached to his original unbelief. There is no difference between one race and another. Perhaps it was that his curse was effective on most of them, not all of them." Bābā at-Tinbuktī, (translated by John Hunwick and Fatima Harrak in *Miʿrāj aṣ-ṣuʿūd*, 2000, pp. 30-31).

13 Ibid.

What about slavery in Mauritania

The notion that black Africans were natural slaves seems to have persisted in Muslim thought until as recently as the nineteenth century. Muḥammad as-Sanūsī ibn Ibrāhīm al-Jārimī, in his *Tanbīh ahl aṭ-ṭughyān 'alā ḥurriyyat as-sūdān* ['Counsel to the Tyrannical People Regarding the Freedom of the Blacks'], reports North African attitudes towards black Africans, "I found some of the uncouth Maghribīs (Moroccans) claiming that all blacks without exception were slaves who did not deserve to be free, for how should they deserve that, being black of skin? On this matter they relate fantasies that have no foundation to them in (Islamic) law or the natural order. As for the law, nothing came down from the Lawgiver that would explain why among all peoples they should be enslaved rather than others. With regard to nature, (such an argument is unacceptable) because the natural order rejects blacks being slaves without a compelling legal reason."[14] Moroccan jurist Aḥmad ibn Khālid an-Nāṣirī (d. 1897) wrote an impassioned legal treatise attacking the illegal enslavement of black Africans by Arab and North African Muslims. In the treatise, An-Nāṣirī discusses the concept of slavery in the modern world as well as the rationale behind Islam permitting slavery:

> It will be clear to you from what we have related of the history of the *Sūdān* how far the people of these lands had taken to Islam from ancient times. It will also be clear that they are among the best peoples in regard to Islam, the most religiously upright, the most avid for learning and the most devoted to men of learning. This state of affairs is to be found in most of their kingdoms bordering on the Maghrib, as you are aware.
>
> Thus will be apparent to you the heinousness of the affliction that has beset the lands of the *Maghrib* since ancient times in regard to the indiscriminate enslavement

[14] Hunwick and Powell, 2007, pp. 43-44.

of the people of the *Sūdān* and the importation of droves of them every year to be sold in the market places in town and country, where men trade in them as one would trade in beasts – nay worse than that. People have become so inured to that, generation after generation, that many common folk believe that the reason for being enslaved according to the Holy Law is merely that a man should be black in colour and come from those regions. This, by God's life, is one of the foulest and greatest evils perpetrated upon God's religion, for the people of the *Sūdān* are Muslims having the same rights and responsibilities as ourselves.

Even if you assume that some of them are pagans or belong to a religion other than Islam, nevertheless the majority of them today as in former times are Muslims, and judgement is made according to the majority. Again, even if you suppose that Muslims are not a majority, and that Islam and unbelief claim equal membership there, who among us can tell whether those brought here are Muslims or unbelievers? For the basic assumption in regard to the human species is freedom and lack of any cause for being enslaved. Whoever maintains the opposite is denying the basic principle.

No confidence should be placed in what the slave-traders or dealers say, since it is established and well-known that all sellers lie about their goods when selling them and praise them lavishly for qualities they do not possess. Slave dealers are even more prone to do that. How could we believe them when we see that those who import them or deal in them are men of no morals, no manly qualities, and no religion, and when we know the [evil nature of the] times and see [the wickedness of] their people?

Nor should any reliance be put upon the protestations of a slave man or woman, as the jurists have ruled, since motives and circumstances differ in this regard. A seller may do them so much ill that they would not admit to anything that would affect their sale. Or a slave may have the objective of getting out of the hands of his master by any possible means, thus finding it easy to admit to slave status so that the sale may be promptly effected. Other motives may also exist.

Men of integrity and others have frequently made the point that the people of the *Bilād as-Sūdān* today as in former times make war on one another and kidnap each other's children, enslaving them in places far removed from their tribal homes or inhabited places, and that in this they are like the nomadic Arabs of the Maghrib who raid one another and drive off or steal each other's flocks and herds out of lack of religious principles and the absence of anything that restrains them. How then can a man who has scruples about his religion permit himself to buy something of this nature? How, too, can he allow himself to take their women as concubines considering that this involves entering upon a sexual liaison of dubious legality?

Abū Ḥamid al-Ghazālī, may God be pleased with him, said in the section "The Lawful and the Forbidden" of his *Iḥyā 'Ulūm ad-Dīn* ['The Revival of the Islamic Sciences']: "Be aware that in regard to food brought to you as a gift, or that you wish to purchase or accept as a present, it is not up to you to institute inquiries about it and say that since it is something the lawfulness of which you cannot ascertain you will not take it without inquiring about it. Nor yet should you dispense with inquiry and merely accept all things whose forbidden nature you cannot determine. On the contrary, sometimes inquiry is obligatory, sometimes it is forbidden, sometimes recommended and sometimes objectionable. Therefore a distinction must be made [between the various cases]. The clear rule is that the existence of areas of doubt provides the presumption for inquiry." He went on to explain this at length – may God be pleased with him – and made it clear that if the seller is suspected of trying to promote the sale of his goods, then his word should not be relied on. If this is true about goods, then how much more is it true about the enslavement of human beings and mastery over women's genitalia, for both of which matters the Lawgiver had even greater concern, as is well known from the Holy Law and its sources.

Shaykh Aḥmad Bābā, in the treatise he set forth on this question entitled *Miʿrāj aṣ-Ṣuʿud*, produced an analysis with which he concluded the work, mentioning those tribes of the *Sūdān* who were unbelievers, such as Mossi, some of the Fulani and others. He stated that it was permissible to enslave anybody who came from those tribes. Ibn Khaldūn also said: "Beyond the Nile are a black people called Lamlam. They are unbelievers who brand their faces and their temples." He also said: "The people of Ghana and Takrur raid them, make them captive and sell them to merchants who carry them off to the Maghrib. These people make up the greater part of their slaves and beyond them to the south is no inhabited land of any consequence."

But this analysis which Shaykh Aḥmad Bābā made is only valid insofar as the people of the lands which border them are concerned and those who come across slaves brought from among them and others [beyond them]. As for the people of the Maghrib who are "beyond what is beyond" [in relation to such peoples] and between whom and the land of the *Sūdān* is a wide waterless desert and a wilderness inhabited only by the wind, who can ascertain the facts for them? We have already said that no confidence should be placed upon what the slave-traders say, and who among us can tell whether those tribes still remain pagan? Moreover, people nowadays pay no heed at all to this, and whenever they see a slave put up for sale in the market they go ahead and buy him, ignoring all this. The only questions they put concern bodily defects, and in this matter it makes no difference whether the slave is black or white or any other colour. Worse than that, in these days the evildoer and those who flout God, kidnap freeborn children in the tribes, villages and cities of the Maghrib and sell them openly in the markets without anyone showing resentment or being angered on behalf of the religion. Jews and Christians have begun to buy them and to enslave them with our full knowledge, and this is a punishment to us from God, were we but to reflect. God help us for the affliction which has overtaken us in the matter of our religion.

To sum up: since, as we have said, the basic human condition is freedom, and since it has been known from age to age that the people of *Sūdān* who border on us are mostly or wholly Muslims, and since men of integrity and others have frequently made the point that they make war on each other and kidnap each other's children and sell them unjustly, and we have seen with our own eyes that the slave merchants and dealers are men of no morals and no religion, we should have no hesitation in declaring that anyone who enters into a transaction of this forbidden nature is imperilling his salvation. As for [the argument] that the slave-traders have laid upon them, this is not a sufficient reason in Holy Law to allow one to enter into the purchase of slaves from them, since it is a weak indication [of validity] surrounded by pieces of factual evidence which give it the lie. Let a man therefore question his heart, for the Prophet, may God bless him and grant him peace, said: "Question your heart ... even if they [the jurists] give you a decision."[15] For if one refers to one's heart over this dilemma one can scarcely hesitate over this burning question at all.

And now, leaving all that aside, we would say that even if there were no more than a strong doubt in this matter, coupled with the evilness of the times and frivolity of its people in matters of religion, there would be in these three factors plus a care for preventive action, which is a principle of Holy Law, especially in the view of Mālik, may God be pleased with him, sufficient to oblige one to cease having anything to do with an evil which is derogatory to honour and religion. We ask God to give success to him whom He has charged with the affairs of his servants in bringing to an end this wickedness.

For the reason in Holy Law which existed in the time of the Prophet and the pious forefathers for enslaving people does not exist today; that is being taken prisoner in *jihād* which has as its object to make the word of God supreme and to bring men to His religion which He chose for His servants. This is our religion which was brought to us as law

---

[15] The full text is: Wābiṣah ibn Ma'bad ﷺ said, "I came to the Messenger of Allah ﷺ and he said, 'You have come to ask about goodness (*birr*)?' I said, 'Yes!' He said, 'Ask your heart for a judgement. Goodness is that towards which the self is tranquil and towards which the heart is tranquil. Badness (*ithm*) is that which becomes agitated in the self and it goes agitatedly to and fro in the breast even though people repeatedly give you a judgement [as to a matter's permissibility].'" A good hadith which is narrated in the two *Musnads* of the Imams Aḥmad ibn Ḥanbal and Ad-Dārimī with a good *isnad*. Another narration has: "Ask yourself for a *fatwa* even if the *muftīs* give *fatwa*." Al-Bukhārī narrated it in his *Tārīkh* from Wābiṣah - Ed.

by our Prophet – may God bless him and grant him peace. What is in opposition to it is in opposition to the religion, and what is other than it is something not laid down by Holy Law, and success is in God's hand alone. "*Lord, we have wronged ourselves, and if You do not pardon us and have mercy upon us we shall be among those who suffer [eternal] loss.*[16]"[17]

---

[16] Sūrat al-A'rāf 7:23.

[17] An-Nāṣirī, 1955, pp. 131-134, (translated by John Hunwick and Eve Trout Powell in *The African Diaspora in the Mediterranean Lands of Islam*, 2007, pp. 44-48).

6

Benefits of Brown and Dark Skin

Although Islam teaches racial equality, there is sometimes a sharp contrast between the teachings of Islam and the practices of Muslims. Contrary to Arnold Toynbee and many historians' view of racial attitudes in pre-modern Muslim societies, the perception that 'white' Muslims "have always been free from colour-prejudice *vis-á-vis* the non-white races," is a slight exaggeration.[1] The amount of evidence of anti-black sentiment found in classical Arab-Muslim literature indicates colourism was sometimes very much a serious issue in Muslim societies.[2] Despite this, at no time did the Muslims ever

---

[1] Abdul Aziz al-Khayyaat says, "We don't find the practice of racial discrimination and the politics of bigotry in Arab or Islamic countries." Al-Khayyaat, 2002, p. 75. Paul Hardy says in his study of race and Islam, "Although Islamic society was multi-racial from the beginning, in none of the regions where the religion became dominant did the concept of race enter Muslim consciousness." Hardy, 2002, p. 1. 'Abd al-'Azīz 'Abd al-Qādir Kāmil echoes a similar sentiment in *Islam and the Race Question*, 1970.

[2] Classical Arab-Muslim literature like *One Thousand and One Nights*, depicts blacks in various hostile stereotypes. Initially the theme of darkness/blackness in Islamic literature had nothing to do with skin colour but over time it became associated with racial representations. See Bernard Lewis, 'The African Diaspora and the Civilisation of Islam', in Kilson, 1976, *The African Diaspora*, pp. 48-49.

practice the kind of racial oppression which existed until recently in the United States and South Africa.

The idea that in Islam blacks are destined for eternal damnation has been claimed by black orientalists and pan-Africanists of recent times. In *Layers of Blackness*, an interesting exploration of colourism in the African diaspora, Deborah Gabriel quotes the following Qur'ānic verse as an example of "racist attitudes in Islam". *"On the Day when faces are whitened and faces are blackened. As for those whose faces are blackened: 'What! Did you become kāfir after having had īmān? Taste the punishment for your kufr!' As for those whose faces are whitened, they are in Allah's mercy, remaining in it timelessly, for ever."*[3] Commenting on the above-mentioned verse, Gabriel says the concept of blackness (and black skin) in the Qur'ān is "synonymous with evil".[4] Contrary to her view, the Qur'ān emphatically rejects the concept of racism. Differences of colour in creation reflect the grandeur of the Creator. Brown and dark skin, like other hues, are signs to reflect on. Only those who are firmly established in sound knowledge can grasp this, as the Qur'ān says, *"Among His signs is the creation of the heavens and the earth and the variety of your languages and colours. There are certainly signs in that for every being."*[5] There is another explicit passage in the Qur'ān that has a direct bearing on Islam's stance towards race and colour: *"Do you not see that Allah sends down water from the sky and by it We bring forth fruits of varying colours? And in the mountains there are streaks of white and red, of varying shades, and rocks of deep jet black. And mankind and beasts and livestock are likewise of varying colours. Only those of His slaves with knowledge have fear of Allah. Allah is Almighty, Ever-Forgiving."*[6] Human skin complexions are insignificant to Allah, as the Prophet ﷺ said, "Allah, exalted is He, does not look at your appearances and your

---

[3] Sūrah Āli 'Imrān 3:106-107.

[4] Gabriel, 2007, pp.16-17.

[5] Sūrat ar-Rūm 30:22.

[6] Sūrah Fāṭir 35:27-28.

possessions, rather He only looks at your hearts and your deeds."[7] Differences in human pigmentation were created for wise purposes which only Allah, the All-Wise, knows in their entirety. Leading dermatologists have conducted research into some of the benefits of and wisdom in brown and dark skin, which are presented below.[8]

1. Radiant youthful looking skin – Brown and dark skin has more melanin, thus resulting in a warmer more beautiful skin shade. Brown skin is naturally warm with a glowing complexion ranging from yellow to olive to deep chocolate brown. Melanin guards brown and dark skin from the long-term damage associated with ageing – the development of deep wrinkles, rough surface texture, and age spots (sometimes called liver spots). Thus brown/dark-skinned people seem to age more slowly than fair-skinned people.
2. Protection against cancer – Brown and dark skin helps protect against skin cancer which develops as a result of ultraviolet light radiation, causing mutations in the skin. Dark skin prevents radiation of UV-A rays from destroying the essential folic acid (or folate), derived from B vitamins.
3. Health – In the absence of modern medicine and diet, a person with dark skin in the tropics (as in Africa) would live longer, be healthier and more likely to reproduce than a person with fair skin.

---

7 Ibn Mājah, *kitāb az-zuhd, bāb al-qanā'ah*, No. 4143; Aḥmad, *musnad Abī Hurayrah*, and Muslim, *kitāb al-birr wa'ṣ-ṣilah wa'l-ādāb, bāb taḥrīm ẓulm al-muslim wa khadhlihi wa'ḥtiqārihi wa damihi wa 'irḍihi wa mālihi*, No. 2564.

8 See Susan C. Taylor, 2008, *Brown Skin: Dr. Susan C. Taylor's prescription for flawless skin, hair, and nails.*

7

Virtues of Blacks and North Africans

Africa has an illustrious place in Islamic history: Abyssinia was the land of the first migration in Islam as well as being the origin of several of the Companions of the Messenger of Allah ﷺ. The Prophet ﷺ instructed his Companions to seek refuge in the land of Abyssinia under the protection of the righteous ruler, the Negus.[1] There are several verses from the Qur'ān praising the Abyssinians[2] and the Prophet ﷺ assigned the *adhān* (call to prayer) to them.[3] He also urged

---

1 When the Messenger of Allah ﷺ saw the affliction of his Companions by the Makkan idolators, he said to them, "If you were to go to Abyssinia (it would be better for you), for the king (i.e. the Negus) will not tolerate injustice and it is a friendly country, until such a time as Allah shall relieve you from your distress." Ibn Isḥāq, 2007, p. 146.

2 As-Suyūṭī reports that the following Qur'ānic verse was revealed about the Negus and his Abyssinian Companions: *"When they listen to what has been sent down to the Messenger, you see their eyes overflowing with tears because of what they recognise of the truth."* Sūrat al-Mā'idah 5:83, As-Suyūṭī, 2004, p. 25.

3 Abū Hurayrah narrates the Prophet ﷺ to have said, "Kingship (*al-mulk*) lies with Quraysh, the judiciary is best executed by the *Anṣār*, the call to prayer (*al-adhān*) is for the Abyssinians and the trust is best kept by the people of Azd (the Yemenis)." At-Tirmidhī, *kitāb al-manāqib, bāb faḍl al-Yaman,* No. 3969; Aḥmad, *musnad Abī Hurayrah,* and As-Suyūṭī, 2004, p. 18. Other versions of the hadith have the words *al-a'immah* (the imams) and *al-khilāfah* (caliphate) instead of *al-mulk* (kingship).

his Companions to treat blacks well.[4] Despite this, in clear contrast to the noble teachings of Islam, xenophobic material can be found in classical Arab-Muslim literature describing the 'ugly' and 'immoral' qualities of black Africans.[5] Many of these portrayals were derived from the writings of the Ancient Greeks, notably the philosophy of Aristotle and the ethnographic theory of Claudius Ptolemaeus (known as Ptolemy in English). According to Ptolemy, the inhabited world was divided into seven latitudinal 'zones' or 'climes', the first being closest to the equator and the seventh near the Arctic Circle. The middle zone (the third and the fourth) corresponded to the Mediterranean lands, and was considered to be the most moderate and ideal zone. Those who inhabited this zone were considered to be the most civilised and intelligent. The farther away one went from this region, the more extreme the climate was, and extreme cold in the north and extreme heat in the south were said to have produced individuals who were distorted mentally and physically. Thus, in this classical Greek perspective both the black people of Africa and the white people of Northern Europe were considered far from the median ideal of human form. The peoples of zones one (sub-Saharan Africa) and seven (Scandinavia) were regarded as savages with deviant lifestyles. The ancient heritage of the Greeks and the Hamitic myth were appropriated by Arab and Persian Muslims as they expanded around the Mediterranean and established schools of translation, teaching

---

4 Ibn Hishām reported that the Prophet ﷺ said, "Show piety in dealing with the protected peoples, those of the settled lands, the blacks, the crinkly haired, for they have a noble ancestor and marriage ties (with us, i.e. Arabs)." Ibn Hishām relates this report in his annotated notes on Ibn Isḥāq's biography of the Prophet ﷺ. Ibn Isḥāq, 2007, p. 691.

5 "In both Arab and Iranian Islamic writings, blacks are accused of being stupid, untruthful, vicious, cowardly, sexually unbridled, ugly and distorted, excessively merry, and easily affected by food and drink," says Minoo Southgate in his study of the representation of blacks in classical Arab and Persian literature. For a full discussion, see Minoo Southgate, 'The negative images of blacks in some Medieval Iranian writings' in *Iranian Studies*, 17, 1984, pp. 3-36.

and research in Baghdad and other centres of learning. The Ptolemaic framework is very much present in the thinking of the famed North African sociologist of the fourteenth century Ibn Khaldūn.[6] Other Muslim writers such as Al-Mas'ūdī,[7] Ibn al-Faqīh[8] and Al-Maqdiṣī[9] invoked the myth and stereotypes of Ḥām in their works, displaying antagonism towards blacks and their culture. This racist material led to many misconceptions about Islam's perception of blacks, in sharp

---

6 Ibn Khaldūn discusses at length the 'natural' dispositions of the various peoples in the world. About blacks he says, "The blacks are, as a rule, submissive to slavery, because they have little that is essentially human and possess attributes that are quite similar to those of dumb animals." Ibn Khaldūn, (translated by Franz Rosenthal), 2005, p. 117.

7 Al-Mas'ūdī quotes Galen, "(there are) Ten specific attributes of the black man, which are all found in him and in no other: frizzy hair, thin eyebrows, broad nostrils, thick lips, pointed teeth, smelly skin, black eyes, furrowed hands and feet, a long penis and great merriment. Galen says that merriment dominates the black man because of his defective brain, whence also the weakness of his intelligence." Al-Mas'ūdī, 1966, p. 91.

8 Ibn al-Faqīh, a tenth century Persian historian and geographer, reports in *Mukhtaṣar kitāb al-buldān* ['The Abridgement of the Book of the Lands']: A man of discernment said, "The people of Iraq have sound minds, commending passions, balanced natures, and high proficiency in every art, together with well-proportioned limbs, well-compounded humours, and a pale brown colour. They are the ones who are done to a turn in the womb. They do not come out with something between blond, buff, balanced, and leprous colouring, such as the infants dropped from the wombs of the women of the Slavs and other similar light complexion; nor are they overdone in the womb until they are burned, so that the child comes out something between black, murky, malodorous, stinking, and crinkly-haired, with uneven limbs, deficient minds, and depraved passions, such as the *Zanj*, Abyssinians, and other blacks who resemble them. The Iraqis are neither half-baked dough nor burned crust, but between the two." Ibn al-Faqīh, 1885, p. 162, (translated by Bernard Lewis in *Islam, Volume II: Religion and Society,* 1987, p. 209).

9 Describing the *Bujja*, an ethnic group amongst the blacks, Al-Maqdiṣī says, "It is said that there is no marriage among them, that the child does not know his father, and that they eat people," and "The *Zanj* are people of black colour, with flat noses, kinky hair, and little understanding or intelligence." Al-Maqdiṣī, 1903, iv, pp. 69-70, (translated by Bernard Lewis in *Islam, Volume II: Religion and Society,* 1987, p. 110).

contrast to the teachings of the Prophet ﷺ. Ibn Hishām reported that the Prophet ﷺ said, "Show piety in dealing with the protected peoples, those of the settled lands, the blacks, the crinkly haired, for they have a noble ancestor and marriage ties (with us, i.e. Arabs)."[10] 'Umar, the freed slave of Ghafrah, explained that by ancestry the Prophet ﷺ was referring to the fact that the Prophet Ismā'īl's عليه السلام mother (Hājar) was Egyptian, and the marital tie was contracted when the Prophet ﷺ had a son by an Egyptian, Māriyah the Copt. As-Suyūṭī narrates on the authority of Ibn 'Abbās رضي الله عنه that the Prophet ﷺ said, "Follow the blacks, for among them are three of the masters of Paradise; Luqmān the Wise, the Negus and Bilāl the *mu'adhdhin.*"[11]

In defence of black people, medieval Muslim writers like Al-Jāḥiẓ, Ibn al-Jawzī, Ibn Baṭṭūṭah and As-Suyūṭī produced works cataloguing some of the virtues of black people.[12] The following is a collection of some of these virtues mentioned in their works. Al-Jāḥiẓ says about blacks in *Fakhr as-sūdān 'alā al-bīḍān*, "There is a general agreement that among no other people is generosity so widespread and deep-rooted as it is among blacks. A quality found only among noble people! Blacks have a natural sense of rhythm, dance and drum beat. They are also the best singers. No other people have such fine, reso-

---

[10] Ibn Hishām relates this report in his annotated notes on Ibn Isḥāq's biography of the Prophet ﷺ. Ibn Isḥāq, 2007, p. 691.

[11] Ibn 'Asākir relates this hadith in his biography of Bilāl. As-Suyūṭī, 2004, p. 17. Ibn al-Jawzī said that this hadith is not authentic. Ibn Ḥibbān said that the text of this tradition is erroneous. Ibn al-Jawzī, 2008, p. 471.

[12] Ibn Baṭṭūṭah, the famous scholar and traveller, wrote of sub-Saharan Africa in a vastly different light in comparison to his predecessors. Of all the medieval travel writers, Ibn Baṭṭūṭah was the only one who actually travelled to both East Africa and West Africa. Most Arab and Persian authors who spoke disparagingly of black Africans had never travelled to sub-Saharan Africa themselves, and their tales were largely based on hearsay. There were other Muslim historians and geographers such as Ibn Rustah, Al-Iṣṭakhrī and Isḥāq ibn al-Ḥusayn who described the 'Land of the Blacks', *Bilād as-Sūdān*, fairly. See Ibn Rustah, 1892, p. 102; Al-Iṣṭakhrī, 1870, p. 40; and Al-Ya'qūbī, 1892, pp. 334-337, 345.

nant voices or more natural sounding and eloquent speech. They are unique among the peoples of the world. Stammering, stuttering and speech impediments do not exist among them. Certain black orators can, in the presence of kings, speak from sunrise to sunset, without pause or hesitation. No race on Earth possesses such strength and stamina. Blacks are physically stronger than other peoples; a single black man can lift a boulder that would defeat a group of Arabs or any other race. They are courageous, energetic and generous too. Blacks are always cheerful, laughing and full of life, all of which are signs of a noble character."[13] Virility is another virtue that the blacks possess according to Al-Jāḥiẓ; he lauds the high sexual potency of the blacks and their ability to sire a great number of children.[14] Ibn al-Jawzī says, "Among the blacks' virtues are strength and willpower which produce courage." Ibn al-Jawzī adds, "The Abyssinians are known for their abundant generosity, excellent manners, inoffensiveness, cheerfulness, eloquence, ease of expression and diction."[15] Ibn Baṭṭūṭah spoke highly about the black Africans he met on his journey through Africa, "They are strict in observing the prayers, studying the religious law, and memorising the Qur'ān."[16] An-Nāṣirī lavishly praises blacks in his chronicle of North Africa, "They are among the best peoples in regard to Islam, the most religiously upright, the most avid for learning and the most devoted to men of learning."[17]

The peoples of North Africa comprise two main ethnic groups: Berbers and Coptic Egyptians. The Berbers, who know themselves as Amāzigh, are the indigenous people of North Africa, and today the majority of Berbers live in Morocco and Algeria, but they also include

---

13 Al-Jāḥiẓ, 2000, vol. 1, pp. 138-139.
14 Al-Jāḥiẓ, 2000, vol. 1, p. 154.
15 Ibn al-Jawzī, 1998, p. 40.
16 Ibn Baṭṭūṭah, 2004, p. 284.
17 An-Nāṣirī, 1955, (translated by John Hunwick and Eve Trout Powell in *The African Diaspora in the Mediterranean Lands of Islam*, 2007, p. 44).

Saharan tribes such as the Tuareg. The region they inhabit is known as *al-Maghrib*, 'The West'. The language of the Berbers belongs to the Afro-Asiatic language family and it can be broken down into three hundred different dialects. The distinguishing physical characteristics of Berbers are a slight build, and their skin tone varies from white, to near-white, to dark brown. The Berbers have intermingled with many ethnic groups, most commonly the Arabs. The Berber revolt in the eighth century led to great hostility within the Muslim community towards the Berbers. In direct contravention of Islamic law, the Berbers were subjugated to extraordinary levies and harsh policies by Umayyad governors. As a result, resentful Berbers grew receptive to radical *Kharijite* activists. To discredit the Berbers, forged prophetic traditions and disparaging stories of the Berbers quickly followed. A tradition falsely attributed to the Prophet ﷺ says, "There are seventy parts of wickedness. The Berbers possess sixty-nine whilst the Jinn possess one."[18] Many Berbers initially resisted Islam, but once they accepted the religion, many became influential warriors, scholars and strong advocates for Islam. The Almoravid (*al-Murābiṭūn*) and Almohad (*al-Muwaḥḥidūn*) dynasties of North Africa and Islamic Spain were Berbers. Under the rule of Berber Muslims, civilisation, culture and the arts flourished spectacularly. Berbers are a proud people, full of culture and immense courage. Speaking of the Berbers, Ibn Khaldūn, the great Arab historian said, "They belong to a powerful, formidable, brave and numerous people; a true people like so many others the world has seen, like the Arabs, the Persians, the Greeks and the Romans. The men who belong to this family of peoples have inhabited the *Maghrib* since the beginning of time."[19] Just as Al-Jāḥiẓ had done, Ibn García defiantly challenged the presupposed superiority of Arabs. In his controversial *shu'ūbiyyah* epistle, Ibn García heaped

[18] Ibn al-Jawzī, 2008, pp. 472–474.

[19] Brett, 1997, p. 1.

praise on non-Arabs like the Berbers for their tenacity, bravery and culture.[20] Ibn Baṭṭūṭah also made mention of the piety of the Berbers in his travel diary.[21]

Prior to the Muslim conquest of Egypt in the seventh century, the Egyptians were referred to as Copts (*al-Qibṭ*) or as Coptic. Since then, the word 'Coptic' has undergone a semantic shift over the centuries to refer specifically to Egyptian Christians. The Copts are highly regarded in Islam, with some notable personalities among them. Hājar, the mother of the Prophet Ismā'īl ﷺ and wife of the Prophet Ibrāhīm ﷺ, was Coptic. Māriyah, the mother of the last-born child of the Prophet Muḥammad ﷺ, was also a Copt. When the Companions set forth to battle, the Prophet ﷺ instructed them to treat the Copts amicably, as they were his blood relations, "You will open Egypt [to Islam], and that is a land in which the Carat (*qīrāṭ*) is spoken of, so when you have opened it [to Islam] treat its people well, for they have a covenant and share blood relations (with us)" or he said, "a covenant and in-lawship."[22] In another narration, the Messenger of Allah ﷺ praised the Copts for their strength and said they will help spread Islam, "Indeed you are going to come upon a people with curly hair, I urge you to treat them well. For they are a people of strength and will reach your enemies by the permission of Allah," meaning the Copts of Egypt.[23]

---

20 Ibn García (Gharsiyah) the Basque (al-Bashkunsī), a leading proponent and advocate of *shu'ūbiyyah* thought in al-Andalus, wrote a famous epistle attacking the Arabs for their overt discrimination against non-Arabs. See Larsson, 2003, *Ibn García's Shu'ūbiyya Letter: Ethnic and Theological Tensions in Medieval al-Andalus.*

21 Ibn Baṭṭūṭah, 2002, pp. 3-24.

22 Muslim, *kitāb faḍā'il aṣ-ṣaḥābah, bāb waṣiyyah an-Nabiyyi ṣalla'llāhu 'alayhi wa sallama bi ahl Miṣr,* No. 2543.

23 *Musnad Abī Ya'lā, musnad 'Amr ibn Ḥarīth,* No. 1473. Abū Ya'lā says, "Its narrators are trustworthy."

8

Interracial Marriages

The Messenger of Allah ﷺ said, "Women are married for four reasons: their wealth and for their standing, their beauty and for their *dīn*. Gain one who has *dīn*, may your hands be dusty!"[1] In another tradition, the Prophet ﷺ was reported to have said, "Do not marry women for their beauty for perhaps their beauty may ruin them, and do not marry them for their wealth for perhaps their wealth may make them disobedient, but instead marry them for their *dīn*. A black slave woman with a perforated nose who has the *dīn* is better."[2] There are several examples of the Messenger of Allah ﷺ urging his Companions to marry women of colour because of their *dīn*. One day, he ﷺ informed his Companions, "Whoever wishes to marry a woman

1 Al-Bukhārī, *kitāb an-nikāḥ, bāb al-akfā' fī ad-dīn*, No. 4802; Muslim, *ar-raḍā', bāb istiḥbāb nikāḥ dhāt ad-dīn*, No. 1466. A large number of other scholars narrate it. In a similar hadith, the Prophet ﷺ added, "Marry a woman who has *dīn* and good character, may your hands be dusty!" Ibn Ḥibbān, *dhikru mā yustaḥabbu lil-mar'i 'inda't-tazwīj an yaṭluba'd-dīn dūna'l-māl fi'l-'aqd 'alā waladihi aw 'alā nafsih*, No. 4035. "May your hands be dusty!" is an expression that came to have the sense of exhortation - Ed.

2 Ibn Mājah, No. 1859; Al-Bayhaqī 7:80, No. 13247; 'Abd ibn Ḥamīd p. 133, No. 328; Al-Bazzār 6:413, No. 2438. Very weak hadith. Al-Būṣīrī said one of the narrators in this *isnād*, Al-Ifrīqī (full name 'Abd ar-Raḥman ibn Ziyād ibn An'am ash-Sh'abānī) is weak.

from the people of the Garden, let him marry Umm Ayman."[3] Upon hearing this, Zayd ibn Hārithah married her. On another occasion, the Companion 'Abdullāh ibn Rawāḥah became so angry with his black slave-girl that he struck her violently. 'Abdullāh ibn Rawāḥah was so upset by what he had done that he went to the Prophet ﷺ to inform him about what had occurred. The Messenger of Allah ﷺ said, "Tell me about this woman?" 'Abdullāh ibn Rawāḥah replied, "She fasts, she prays, performs her ablutions vigilantly and bears witness that there is no god but Allah and that you are the Messenger of Allah ﷺ." The Prophet ﷺ said "'Abdullāh, she is a believer!" 'Abdullāh said, "By the One Who sent you with the truth, I will definitely set her free and marry her!" which he subsequently did. Some people from amongst the Muslims began to insult 'Abdullāh for marrying a former slave, some others wanted to intermarry with the idolators, hoping for status. The following Qur'ānic verse was revealed informing the faithful that an unattractive slave woman is better than a beautiful free-born idolatrous woman. *"Do not marry women of the idolators until they have īmān. A slave-girl who is one of the believers is better for you than a woman of the idolators, even though she may attract you."*[4] Before colourism penetrated some Muslims' psyches, in early Islam interracial relationships were common; many Companions married women of different races and ethnicities. The mother of the last son of the Prophet ﷺ, Māriyah the Copt, was Egyptian. The former slave Bilāl, who was a black African, married 'Abd ar-Raḥmān ibn 'Awf's sister who was an Arab of good standing. Khālid ibn Rabāḥ al-Ḥabashī, a black Abyssinian, married an Arab woman after Bilāl interceded on his behalf. Sālim, the freed Persian slave of Abū Ḥudhayfah, married Fāṭimah bint al-Walīd ibn 'Utbah, Abū Ḥudhayfah's niece. Fāṭimah bint Qays married Usāmah

3 Ibn Sa'd, 8:224.

4 Sūrat al-Baqarah 2:221, Ibn Kathīr, 2000, p. 275 in *tafsīr* of the aforementioned *āyah*.

ibn Zayd, the son of the aforementioned Umm Ayman, an Abyssinian woman, at the recommendation of the Prophet ﷺ. The cousin of the Prophet ﷺ, Ibn 'Abbās, used to enjoy conjugal relations with his black concubines. Sa'd al-Aswad and Julaybīb, who were reported to have been extremely dark in complexion, both married fair-skinned Arab women with the support of the Prophet ﷺ. 'Abdullāh ibn Abū Bakr (son of the first Caliph of Islam) was reported to have been deeply in love with his black slave-girl.[5] [May Allah be pleased with them all.]

Despite the Prophet's endorsement of interracial marriages and the widespread practice of interracial relations amongst the Companions, some of the early Muslim jurists disapproved of Arabs marrying non-Arabs, basing their edicts on weak and unreliable prophetic traditions prohibiting interracial relations.[6] Some classical jurists, like Aḥmad ibn Naqīb al-Miṣrī (d. 1368), author of the legal treatise, *'Umdat as-sālik wa 'uddat an-nāsik* ['Reliance of the Traveller and Tools of the Worshipper'], considered non-Arabs to be unsuitable marriage partners for Arabs because of their lineage.[7] The Hindu caste system also managed to infiltrate the thinking of Muslims from the Indian sub-continent. When the Muslims went to India and started

---

5 Ibn al-Jawzī, 1998, pp. 233-245.

6 "Marry like with like and match like with like. Choose carefully for your offspring, and beware of the *Zanjī*, for he is a distorted creature," (Ibn Ḥibbān in *aḍ-ḍu'afā'* – weak hadith – from 'Ā'ishah ﷺ); "Arabs are the equals of Arabs (in marriage suitability), and the *mawālī* are the equal of the *mawālī*, except for weavers and cuppers," (*Sunan al-Bayhaqī* from 'Ā'ishah ﷺ); "O *mawālī*! The wrongdoers among you are those who intermarry with Arabs. O Arabs! The wrongdoers among you are those who marry with *mawālī*." (Abū Nu'aym narrated it from 'Utbah ibn Ṭuway' al-Māzinī). Al-Muttaqī, 1895, viii, pp. 24-28.

Mawālī comprise both those people who, while accepting Islam, enter into a client relationship (*walā'*) with the person with whom they accepted Islam and his tribe, and freed slaves who also have a client relationship (*walā'*) with the persons who set them free – Ed.

7 The Shafi'ite school of jurisprudence disapproved of non-Arab men marrying Arab women, citing the prophetic tradition, "Allah has chosen the Arabs above others...." Ibn an-Naqīb, 2008, pp. 523-524.

preaching Islam, many Hindus converted to Islam from the various 'castes'. Since the Hindu caste system was prevalent in India, many of the convert Muslims kept their cultural practices and beliefs in the caste system when selecting a marital partner.[8] Despite Islam's teaching of racial equality, some South Asian Muslim scholars have tried to justify an ethnic caste hierarchy within Islam and disapproved of marriages with black Muslims. Al-Jāḥiẓ, the great Muslim scholar of East African descent, was greatly troubled by the endogamy of some of the Arabs of his time. He said, "It is part of your ignorance that in pre-Islamic times you regarded us as good enough to marry your women, yet when the justice of Islam came, you considered this no longer valid, and you found us distasteful, though the desert was full of our people who married your women, who were rulers and leaders, who defended your honour and saved you from your enemies!"[9]

Following the clear instruction from the Qur'ān, Imam Mālik, the eponymous jurist of the Mālikī school of Islamic jurisprudence, disagreed with many of the jurists of his time and permitted interracial marriages, asserting that all human beings are equal and marriages may be contracted without any consideration for ethnicity or lineage. According to Mālik, *taqwā* (piety and righteous conduct) is the only criterion in judging a person's suitability for marriage. He cited as evidence for his judgement the Qur'ānic verse, *"The noblest among you in Allah's sight is the one with the most taqwā (atqā)."*[10] The verse proclaims the primacy of *taqwā*[11] over racial and tribal distinction. Mālik argued that *taqwā* is the only valid criteria in judging the *kafā* (marriage suitability) of a potential spouse; he felt

---

8 Madani, 1993, pp. 116-131.

9 Al-Jāḥiẓ, 2000, vol. 1, p. 139.

10 Sūrat al-Ḥujurāt 49:13.

11 Ibn Juzayy al-Kalbī says in his *tafsīr*: "*Taqwā* is a verbal noun which derives from *wiqāyah* (preserving, guarding). Its meaning is fear, clinging to obedience to Allah and abandoning disobedience of Him. It is the sum of all good." - Ed.

that a person's lineage, wealth and occupation are irrelevant.[12] This sound legal opinion is consistent with the clear instruction of the Prophet ﷺ, "If someone comes to you (to ask for your daughter's hand in marriage) with whose character and *dīn* you are pleased, then you should marry him to her. *If you do not do so, there will be discord in the land and widespread corruption.*[13]"[14]

[12] Al-Qarāfī, 2008, vol. 4, pp. 22-27; Ash-Shaqafah, 2007, vol. 3, pp. 207-224; Ibn 'Abd al-Barr, 2007, pp. 307-310; Al-Gharyānī, 2002, pp. 506-511.

[13] See Sūrat al-Anfāl 8:73: "*If you do not act in this way there will be turmoil in the land and great corruption.*" - Ed.

[14] At-Tirmidhī, *abwāb an-nikāḥ 'an rasūlillāh ṣalla'llāhu 'alayhi wa sallam, bāb mā jā'a fī man tarḍawna dīnahu wa khuluqahu*, No. 1091; Ibn Mājah, *kitāb an-nikāḥ, bāb al-akfā'*, No. 1967; Al-Ḥākim, No. 2695; Ash-Shaqafah, 2007, pp. 207–224.

9

The Elevated Status of Black Africa in Islam

In the highly controversial *The Destruction of Black Civilisation*, Chancellor Williams casts several aspersions upon Arabs and the religion of Islam. Williams' inaccurate portrayal of Islam and its stance towards black Africans subsequently led scores of Pan-Africanists and antagonists of Islam to attack the religion that liberated Africa. Williams' charge that Islam "subjugated (Africa and) the blacks" is patently false. Africa flourished after the advent of Islam, producing great civilisations and highly acclaimed educational institutions as historical records testify. The sources for the history of Islam in Africa divide themselves into two categories: external and internal; and these again subdivide: the external into the Islamic and European, and the internal into oral and written. The numerous external Islamic works are the most reliable and factual sources for the history of Africa. Although these works constitute the primary source for African history, they contain some inauthentic reports and certain prejudices about black people. Nevertheless they are still the most useful source for African history.[1]

1 For a contemporary study of Black Africa see Cheikh Anta Diop, 1987, *Pre-Colonial Black Africa* and Basil Davidson, 1995, *Africa in History.*

In early Muslim literature, black Africans are either referred to as *Ḥabash* (Abyssinians) or *Sūdān* (Blacks). After Islam began to spread into Africa, other and more specific terms were added, the commonest being *Nūba*, *Bujja* and *Zanj*. The term *Bilād as-Sūdān* (lands of the Blacks) is applied in classical Arabic usage to the whole area of Black Africa south of the Sahara; sometimes it is used for the south and south-east Asia region inhabited by relatively dark-skinned people. Arab Muslim historians began to write about West Africa at the beginning of the eighth century. The famous scholar Ibn Munabbih (d. 737) wrote as early as the mid-eighth century, followed by the great Arab historian and geographer, Al-Mas'ūdī's (d. 956) *Murūj adh-dhahab wa ma'ādin al-jawāhir* ['Meadows of Gold and Mines of Gems'] in 947. Early Muslim geographers like Muḥammad ibn Mūsā al-Khwārizmī (d. 850) and Muḥammad Abū al-Qāsim ibn Ḥawqal[2] wrote about African territories and lifestyles, both under the title *Ṣūrat al-arḍ* ['The Image of the Earth']. More copious material on sub-Saharan Africa is available from Abū 'Abdullāh al-Bakrī (d. 1094), an Andalusian scholar, who left us a precious description of Ancient Ghana in 1067 with his *Kitāb al-masālik wa'l-mamālik* ['The Book of Highways and Kingdoms']. In 1154, Al-Idrīsī (d. 1165), one of the greatest medieval chroniclers, described Ghana as "the greatest country in the land of *Sūdān*, the most populous, and having the most extensive trade."[3] The encyclopaedias of the Muslim world compiled by Abū al-Fidā and Yāqūt al-Ḥamawī (*Mu'jam al-Buldān*) provide material on the cultural geography of Black Africa. The Syrian historian, Shihāb ad-Dīn Aḥmad ibn Faḍlillāh al-'Umarī (d. 1384) wrote an encyclopaedia for bureaucrats, which included a description of Ancient Mali and the famous pilgrimage of Mansa Mūsā. Ibn Baṭṭūṭah (d. 1369), the great fourteenth century world traveller, reported the facility and safety with which traders and foreigners

---

[2] He wrote his book in 977CE - Ed.

[3] Segal, 2001, p. 89.

were able to move about, the flourishing agriculture and commerce, and the strict administration of justice in West Africa. Ibn Baṭṭūṭah's chronicle provides an important insight into the life and culture of sub-Saharan Africa in the fourteenth century. When Timbuktu became a famous seat of learning in West Africa, it attracted a large number of scholars who came and lived in the quarters adjacent to the main mosque. Some works of that period have come down to us while many are lost. Ibn Khaldūn (d. 1406) gave us a brief dynastic history of Mali in his history of Islamic civilisation. The sixteenth century travel writer, Al-Ḥassān ibn Muḥammad al-Wazzān al-Fāsī, also known as Leo Africanus (d. 1554), wrote *Waṣf al-Ifrīqiyyah* ['Description of Africa'], an important source on black African history prior to the European invasion. The African Muslim scholar, Maḥmūd Ka'ti, began to write his magnum opus *Kitāb al-Fattāsh* ['The Book of Seekers'] in 1519 but died before it was completed. His son, Ibn al-Mukhtār, completed the book in the year 1565. The work provides us with rich material on the Askiya dynasty of the Muslim empire of Songhay of West Africa. The other famous work of African history is *Tārīkh as-Sūdān* ['History of Black Africa'] (1665) by the African scholar 'Abd ar-Raḥmān as-Sa'dī. 'Abd ar-Raḥmān as-Sa'dī's *Tārīkh as-Sūdān* and Leo Africanus' work are arguably the most comprehensive and accurate accounts of Africa in pre-colonial times.

PART II

10

Prophets

There have reportedly been 124,000 prophets sent by Allah to mankind. Some of these prophets are mentioned in the Qur'ān, *"There are Messengers We have already told you about and Messengers We have not told you about."*[1] Interpreting this verse, 'Alī ibn Abī Ṭālib ﷺ said, "Allah sent a black Abyssinian as a prophet. This man was amongst those prophets whose story was not narrated to the Prophet Muḥammad ﷺ (in the Qur'ān)."[2] This chapter looks at black prophets from the Islamic literary genre, *Qiṣaṣ al-Anbiyā* ['Stories of the Prophets'].

The Prophet of the People of the Ditch

'Alī ibn Abī Ṭālib ﷺ said, "The prophet of the People of the Ditch was Abyssinian." Ibn al-Jawzī narrates on the authority of 'Alī ibn Abī Ṭālib ﷺ: There was one of the kings who became intoxicated and then slept with his sister. When he sobered and regained consciousness he said to his sister, "Woe to you, how are we going to escape from this calamity?" She replied "Gather the people of your kingdom and inform them that Allah has permitted marriage between siblings.

1 Sūrat an-Nisā' 4:164.

2 As-Suyūṭī, 2004, p. 19.

After the news has spread amongst the people, they will soon forget this legislation. Then summon them and forbid it." The king followed the advice of his sister and went to the people and gave a sermon about this new legislation of the permissibility of incest. The people refused to accept the king's edict. The king called for whips and his guards unsheathed their swords. The people still refused to accept the king's ruling. So he dug a ditch and set it alight. The tyrannical king then threw everyone in the ditch that refused to accept his ruling. Many of the scholars of Qur'ānic exegesis said that the people who were burned in the ditch were Abyssinians.[3,4]

Luqmān the Wise

Luqmān in the Qur'ān

We gave Luqman wisdom (ḥikmah): "Give thanks to Allah. Whoever gives thanks only does so to his own good. Whoever is ungrateful, Allah is Rich Beyond Need, Praiseworthy." When Luqman said to his son, counselling him, "My son, do not associate anything with Allah. Associating others with Him is a terrible wrong." We have instructed man concerning his parents. Bearing him caused his mother great debility and the period of his weaning was two years: "Give thanks to Me and to your parents. I am your final destination. But if they try to make you associate something with Me about which you have no knowledge, do not obey them. Keep company with them correctly and courteously in this world but follow the Way of him who turns to Me.

---

3 Ibn al-Jawzī, 1998, p. 83, Sūrat al-Burūj 85: 5-9.

4 There are four interpretations of the story, two of which may be the same: 1. The story told by the Messenger of Allah ﷺ about the king whose people became 'Muslims' and who he burnt alive; 2. The king who slept with his sister; 3. The Abyssinian followers of an Abyssinian prophet; and 4. Dhu Nuwas, the king of Yemen who became a Jew. This last may agree with the first.

The story of the king who committed incest does not mention Abyssinians or a prophet - Ed.

Then you will return to Me and I will inform you about the things you did." "My son, even if something weighs as little as a mustard-seed and is inside a rock or anywhere else in the heavens or earth, Allah will bring it out. Allah is All-Pervading, All-Aware. My son, establish ṣalāh and command what is right and forbid what is wrong and be steadfast in the face of all that happens to you. That is certainly the most resolute course to follow. Do not avert your face from people out of haughtiness and do not strut about arrogantly on the earth. Allah does not love anyone who is vain or boastful. Be moderate in your tread and lower your voice. The most hateful of voices is the donkey's bray."[5]

Luqmān's Status

Mujāhid interpreted the word *ḥikmah* in the Qur'ānic verse, *"We gave Luqman wisdom (ḥikmah)"* to mean *fiqh* (a deep understanding of the religion), *'aql* (strong intelligence) and *iṣābah* (hitting the mark). 'Ikrimah, As-Sa'dī and Ash-Sha'bī interpreted *ḥikmah* to mean *nubuwwah* (prophethood). Ibn al-Jawzī said, "There is a difference of opinion amongst the *'ulamā'* regarding Luqmān's status and as to whether he was a prophet. The majority say that he was a pious sage and not a prophet. However, Companions and early religious scholars such as 'Ikrimah ibn Abī Jaḥl, Al-Layth ibn Sa'd and Sa'īd ibn al-Musayyib were of the opinion that Luqmān was indeed a prophet.[6]

As-Suyūṭī relates on the authority of 'Abd ar-Raḥmān ibn Yazīd ibn Jābir that the Messenger of Allah ﷺ said, "The masters of *as-Sūdān* (blacks) are four: Luqmān the Abyssinian, the Negus, Bilāl and Muhja'."[7] Ibn 'Abbās said, "Luqmān was an Abyssinian servant who

---

5 Sūrah Luqmān 31:12-19.

6 Ibn al-Jawzī, 1998, p. 97.

7 "Ibn 'Asākir narrated it from 'Abd ar-Raḥmān ibn Yazīd ibn Jābir as a *mursal hadith*. Ibn 'Asākir vol. 10:462." As-Suyūṭī, *Jam' al-Jawāmi'*. Al-Ḥākim narrates it without mention of the Negus in *dhikr Bilāl ibn Rabāh mu'adhdhin Rasūlillāh ṣalla'llāhu 'alayhi wa sallama*, No. 5242. He declared it *ṣaḥīḥ*.

worked as a carpenter." Mujāhid said, "Luqmān was a dark-skinned slave with large lips and coarse feet."[8]

The Prophet Dāwūd and Luqmān

Ibn al-Jawzī narrates on the authority of Makhūl that the first time the Prophet Dāwūd ﷺ heard a wise saying from Luqmān was one time while Dāwūd ﷺ was watching some people having a discussion during which Luqmān remained in complete silence. Dāwūd ﷺ said to Luqmān, "Why don't you say something, as the other people do?" He answered, "Speech is meaningless except in mentioning Allah. Silence is meaningless as well except in thinking about the Day of Rising. The religious person is the one who works in silence, the one who is always grateful and humble and who is always content with what he has and is never distressed. He is not attached to the things of this world, thus he escapes the misfortunes of this life [and escapes] succumbing to his passions and thus becomes free. He is loved by everyone, he is mature in mind and always thinks about the afterlife. People live with him in peace but within himself he always feels troubled." Luqmān's reputation spread far and wide, people would gather around him to learn from his words of wisdom.[9]

Luqmān's Wisdoms

Allah elevated Luqmān the Wise due to his wisdom. When a man who used to know Luqmān before (he was given wisdom by Allah) said, "Are you not the slave of so-and-so who used to herd sheep not so long ago?" Luqmān said, "Yes." The man said, "So what happened to you, to account for that which I now see?" Luqmān said, "The decree of Allah is what happened, because of the fulfilment of trusts, honesty in speech and leaving that which does not concern me."[10] Ibn

---

8 As-Suyūṭī, 2004, pp. 52-54.

9 Ibn al-Jawzī, 1998, p. 100.

10 As-Suyūṭī, 2004, p. 56.

al-Jawzī relates: One day, Luqmān's master ordered him to slaughter a sheep and bring its two best organs. Luqmān slaughtered a sheep and brought the tongue and the heart. Luqmān's master then asked Luqmān to bring the two worst organs. So Luqmān brought the tongue and heart again. Luqmān's master asked, "What is this?" Luqmān replied, "The tongue and the heart are the best organs if the owner is righteous. If the owner is evil, the heart and tongue are the most wicked organs!"[11]

Luqmān's Death

Ibn al-Jawzī narrated: It has reached me that when Luqmān was about to die he cried. His son said to him "Father, what makes you weep?" He replied, "O my beloved son! I am not crying over this world, rather I am crying because of what is in front of me: a very long hard journey, a deep grave and an insurmountable obstacle. I do not know whether the heavy load will be removed from me so that I may make the journey to reach my destination or whether it will remain with me so that I will be driven to Hell with it." Soon thereafter Luqmān died. Ibn al-Jawzī narrates: The place of Luqmān's grave is between the Mosque of Ramlah and the site of the market of Ramlah today. In the vicinity there are seven hundred graves of various prophets who came after Luqmān.[12]

Dhu'l-Qarnayn

Dhu'l-Qarnayn in the Qur'ān

They will ask you about Dhu'l-Qarnayn. Say: "I will tell you something about him." We gave him power and authority on the earth and granted him a way to everything. So he followed a way until he reached the setting of the sun and found it setting in a muddy spring and found a people by it. We said,

---

[11] Ibn al-Jawzī, 1998, p. 97.

[12] As-Suyūṭī, 2004, p. 60; Ibn al-Jawzī, 1998, pp. 102-103.

"Dhu'l-Qarnayn! You can either punish them or else you can treat them with gentleness." He said, "As for those who do wrong, we will punish them and then they will be returned to their Lord and He will punish them with a dreadful punishment. But as for him who has iman and acts rightly, he will receive the best of rewards and we will issue a command, making things easy for him." Then he followed a way until he reached the rising of the sun and found it rising on a people to whom We had not given any shelter from it. Our knowledge encompasses all that happened to him. Then he followed a path until he arrived between the two mountains where he found a people scarcely able to understand speech. They said, "Dhu'l-Qarnayn! Yajuj and Majuj are causing corruption in the land. Can we, therefore, pay tribute to you in return for your constructing a barrier between us and them?" He said, "The power my Lord has granted me is better than that. Just give me a strong helping hand and I will build a solid barrier between you and them. Bring me ingots of iron!" Then, when he had made it level between the two high mountain-sides, he said, "Blow!" and when he had made it a red hot fire, he said, "Bring me molten brass to pour over it." They were, therefore, unable to climb over it nor were they able to make a breach in it. He said, "This is a mercy from my Lord. But when my Lord's promise comes about, He will crush it flat. The promise of my Lord is surely true."[13]

Dhu'l-Qarnayn's Status

Dhu'l-Qarnayn was a right-acting man from ancient times about whom scholars differ, some saying that he was a prophet whilst others saying that he was a sage. He was a descendent of Yāfith, the son of Nūḥ ﵇. Ibn al-Jawzī reports 'Alī ibn Abī Ṭālib ﵁ to have said, "Dhu'l-Qarnayn was black." Mujāhid said, "The kings of the earth are four men: two are believers and two are disbelievers. As for the two believers, they are the Prophet Sulaymān ﵇, the son of the Prophet Dāwūd ﵇, and Dhu'l-Qarnayn. The two disbelievers are Nimrod and Bukht Nasr." Some say that Dhu'l-Qarnayn lived during the time of the

[13] Sūrat al-Kahf 18:83-98.

Prophet Ibrāhīm ﷺ, the Friend of Allah, and died during that period. Another view is that he was Alexander the Great, as Al-Qurṭubī cites from Ibn Hishām's commentary on Ibn Isḥāq's *sīrah.* There are ten opinions amongst the Muslim scholars regarding the epithet *Dhu'l-Qarnayn* (Possessor of the Two Horns):[14]

1. He called his people to Allah and then the people struck him on his *qarn* (horn) from which he died. Some time elapsed then Allah sent him to another people, and he called people to Allah once again. They struck him on his other *qarn* (horn), from which he died. That was two horns (*qarnayn*). This is the opinion of 'Alī ibn Abī Ṭālib ﷺ.
2. He was given the epithet *Dhu'l-Qarnayn* because he travelled to where the sun sets and rises. This opinion was narrated by Abū Sāliḥ on the authority of Ibn 'Abbās.
3. The exterior of his helmet was made out of copper.
4. He saw himself in a dream as if he was falling from the sky to the earth. He then grasped the two horns (*qarnayn*) of the sun. He informed his people about his vision, whereupon they named him *Dhu'l-Qarnayn.*
5. Because he was the king of both the Persians and the Greeks.[15]
6. Because there was something which resembled two horns on his head.
7. Because he had two braids in his hair. This is the opinion of Al-Ḥasan.
8. Because he was the son of noble parents from an honourable family and household.
9. Because two centuries[16] elapsed during his life.
10. Because he travelled in the night and day.

---

[14] Ibn al-Jawzī, 1998, pp. 85-86.
[15] This fits the view of those who say he was Alexander the Great - Ed.
[16] A *qarn* is also a generation or a century as well as a horn - Ed.

11

Male Companions

Bilāl ibn Rabāḥ

Bilāl ibn Rabāḥ was an esteemed Abyssinian Companion of the Messenger of Allah ﷺ. Bilāl was given the honour of calling the Muslims to prayer at the command of the Messenger of Allah ﷺ immediately after its form was shown to some of the Companions in a dream, thus becoming the first *mu'adhdhin* of Islam. Bilāl was known for his loyalty to the Messenger of Allah ﷺ, benign character and unshakable faith. Bilāl is an exemplary model of steadfastness and devotion to the Islamic *dīn*. His story remains the classic and most frequently cited demonstration that in the religion of Islam, the measure of a man is neither his ethnicity, social status or race, but his *taqwā* and conduct.

Description

Bilāl ibn Rabāḥ was very dark in complexion, tall and thin. He had an aquiline nose and a lot of hair. His beard was sparse with some grey hairs.[1] Bilāl was freed by Abū Bakr aṣ-Ṣiddīq, thus he was referred to as Bilāl the *mawlā* (freed slave) of Abū Bakr. His *kunyah* (patronymic) was Abū 'Abdullāh. He was amongst the Makkan-born Abyssinian slaves.[2]

---

[1] Ibn al-Jawzī, 1998, p. 123.

[2] Ibn al-Jawzī, 1998, pp. 122-129.

Bilāl's High Status

'Abdullāh ibn Buraydah narrated that his father said: "One day, the Prophet ﷺ called for Bilāl. When Bilāl arrived he said, 'Bilāl, what is it that you are doing which made you precede me in the Garden? I did not enter the Garden except I heard your footsteps ahead of me....' Bilāl said, 'I have never called the *adhān* without praying two *rak'at* of prayer. Every time something occurs to interrupt my state of *wuḍū'*, I perform *wuḍū'* and pray two *rak'at* of prayer.' So he [the Prophet ﷺ] said, 'It is because of this.'"[3] On another occasion, the Messenger of Allah ﷺ said, "What an excellent person Bilāl is! He is the leader of the leader of the *mu'adhdhins* and no-one will follow him except for a *mu'adhdhin*. And the *mu'adhdhins* will have the longest necks on the Day of Rising."[4] Ibn 'Umar said to Bilāl, "Receive glad tidings Bilāl!" "For what am I to be cheerful about 'Abdullāh?" replied Bilāl. 'Ibn 'Umar said, "I heard the Messenger of Allah ﷺ saying, 'Bilāl will come on the Day of Rising holding a standard. All of the *mu'adhdhins* will follow him until they enter the Garden.'"[5] Mujāhid said, "Seven people were the first to openly declare their Islamic faith: the Messenger of Allah ﷺ, Abū Bakr, Bilāl, Khabbāb, Ṣuhayb, 'Ammār and Sumayyah, the mother of 'Ammār." Anas ibn Mālik said that the Prophet ﷺ said, "There are four forerunners: I am the forerunner of the Arabs, Ṣuhayb is the forerunner of the Greeks, Salmān is the forerunner of the Persians and Bilāl is the forerunner of the Abyssinians."[6] As-Suyūṭī relates on the authority of Anas ibn Mālik: The Messenger of

---

3 Al-Ḥākim, *min kitāb ṣalāt at-taṭawwu'*, No. 1179, *dhikr Bilāl ibn Rabāh mu'adhdhin Rasūlillāh ṣalla'llāhu 'alayhi wa sallama*, No. 5245; At-Tirmidhī, *manāqib Abī Ḥafṣ 'Umar ibn al-Khaṭṭāb raḍiya'llāhu 'anhu*, No. 3772; and Aḥmad, *ḥadīth Buraydah al-Aslamī raḍiya'llāhu 'anhu*.

4 Al-Ḥākim, *dhikr Bilāl ibn Rabāh mu'adhdhin Rasūlillāh ṣalla'llāhu 'alayhi wa sallama*, No. 5244; and As-Suyūṭī, 2004, p. 77.

5 As-Suyūṭī, 2004, p. 78.

6 Al-Ḥākim, *dhikr manāqib Ṣuhayb ibn Sinān mawlā Rasūlillāh ṣalla'llāhu 'alayhi wa sallama*, No. 5715.

Allah ﷺ said, "The Garden yearns for three people: 'Alī, 'Ammār and Bilāl."[7] Ibn Mājah narrates on the authority of Sālim: One day a poet was praising Bilāl ibn 'Abdullāh and then said, "Bilāl ibn 'Abdullāh is the best of the Bilāls." Upon hearing this 'Umar ibn al-Khaṭṭāb ﷺ interjected, "You lie! The Prophet's Bilāl is the best of the Bilāls!"[8] Al-Bukhārī narrated that 'Umar used to say, "Abū Bakr is our master and he set our master free"[9] meaning Bilāl ibn Rabāḥ ﷺ. Al-Ḥākim relates: There was a brother of Bilāl who used to trace his lineage back to the Arabs and claim to be one of them. He went to ask for an Arab woman's hand in marriage. The family of the woman said, "If Bilāl is present, we will marry you to her." Later on Bilāl came and said to the family, "I am Bilāl ibn Rabāḥ and this is my brother and he has bad character and *dīn*. If you wish to marry him to her, then you may. If you wish to refuse his offer, then do so." The family replied, "Whoever's brother you are, we will accept his marriage proposal," so they married the woman to him.[10] Ibn al-Jawzī reports: On the day of the Opening of Makkah [to Islam], the Messenger of Allah ﷺ instructed Bilāl to ascend to the roof of the Ka'bah and summon the people to prayer. It may be that the Prophet ﷺ wanted to make apparent to the people the racial equality of man in Islam. When Bilāl summoned the people to prayer from on top of the Ka'bah, 'Utāb ibn Usayd said, "All praise is due to Allah Who took the soul of Usayd (his father) before this day!" Hārith ibn Hishām said, "Couldn't Muḥammad find anyone other than this black crow to summon the people to prayer?" Suhayl ibn 'Amr said, "If Allah detests a thing, he changes it." As for Abū Sufyān, he said, "As for me, I am not saying anything. Indeed if I were to utter a word, the

---

7 As-Suyūṭī, 2004, p. 76.

8 Ibn Mājah and Aḥmad.

9 Al-Bukhārī, *kitāb faḍā'il aṣ-ṣaḥābah, bāb manāqib Bilāl ibn Rabāḥ mawlā Abī Bakr, raḍiya'llāhu 'anhumā,* No. 3544; and Al-Ḥākim, *dhikr Bilāl ibn Rabāḥ mu'adhdhin Rasūlillāh ṣalla'llāhu 'alayhi wa sallama,* No. 5239.

10 Al-Ḥākim, *dhikr Bilāl ibn Rabāḥ mu'adhdhin Rasūlillāh ṣalla'llāhu 'alayhi wa sallama*, No. 5237.

heavens will bear witness against me and the earth will testify about me!" Soon thereafter the following verse was revealed: *"Mankind! We created you from a male and female, and made you into peoples (shu'ūb) and tribes (qabā'il) so that you might come to know each other. The noblest among you in Allah's sight is the one with the most taqwā. Allah is All-Knowing, All-Aware."*[11]

The Polytheists Persecute Bilāl

Ibn Isḥāq reports:

> The Quraysh showed their enmity to all those who followed the Prophet ﷺ; every clan which contained Muslims attacked them, imprisoning them, and beating them, allowing them no food or drink, and exposing them to the burning heat of Makkah, so as to seduce them from their religion. Some gave way under pressure of persecution, and others resisted them, being protected by God.
>
> Bilāl, who was afterwards freed by Abū Bakr but at that time belonged to one of the tribe of Jumaḥ, being slave-born, was a faithful Muslim, pure of heart. His father's name was Rabāḥ and his mother was Ḥamāmah. Umayyah ibn Khalaf used to bring him out at the hottest part of the day and throw him on his back in the open valley and have a great rock put on his chest; then he would say to him, "You will stay here until you die or deny Muḥammad and worship al-Lāt and al-'Uzzā." Bilāl used to say whilst he was enduring this, "One God, one God!"[12]

---

[11] Sūrat al-Ḥujurāt 49:13. There are different opinions amongst the scholars regarding the cause for the revelation for 49:13. Ibn al-Jawzī gives three: 1. Because of an altercation between Thābit ibn Qays and another man; 2. Because of Bilāl; 3. After a black man died, the Messenger of Allah ﷺ performed the ritual burial wash, shrouded him and then buried him. The loss of this man's life deeply affected the Companions. Ibn al-Jawzī, 2002, pp. 1332-6.

[12] He said, "One (*aḥad*)! One!" - Ed.

Ibn Isḥāq reports:

> Hishām ibn 'Urwah told me on the authority of his father: Waraqah ibn Nawfal was passing him while he was being thus tortured and saying, "One! One!" and he said, "One! One! By God, Bilāl." Then he went to Umayyah and those of the tribe of Jumaḥ who had maltreated him, and said, "I swear by God that if you kill him in this way I will make his tomb a shrine." One day Abū Bakr passed by while they were thus ill-treating Bilāl, for his house was among this clan. He said to Umayyah, "Have you no fear of God that you treat this poor fellow like this? How long is it to go on?" He replied, "You are the one who corrupted him, so save him from his plight that you see." "I will do so," said Abū Bakr; "I will exchange a servant of mine for Bilāl." The transaction was carried out, and Abū Bakr took Bilāl and freed him.[13]

First Mu'adhdhin of Islam

Ibn Isḥāq reports:

> When the Prophet was firmly settled in Madīnah and his brethren the *Muhājirūn* (Emigrants) were gathered to him and the affairs of the *Anṣār* (Helpers) were arranged, Islam became firmly established. Prayer was instituted, the alms tax and fasting were prescribed, legal punishments fixed, the forbidden and the permitted prescribed, and Islam took up its abode with them. It was this clan of *Anṣār* (Helpers) who *"have taken up their abode (in the city of the Prophet) and in the faith."*[14] When the Prophet first came, the people gathered to him for prayer at the appointed times without being summoned. At first the Prophet thought of using a

---

[13] Ibn Isḥāq, 2007, pp. 143-144.

[14] Sūrat al-Hashr 59:9.

trumpet like that of the Jews who used it to summon to prayer. Afterwards he disliked the idea and ordered a clapper to be made, so it was duly fashioned to be beaten when the Muslims should pray.

Meanwhile 'Abdullāh ibn Zayd ibn Tha'labah heard a voice in a dream, and came to the Prophet saying, "A phantom visited me in the night. There passed by me a man wearing two green garments carrying a clapper in his hand, and I asked him to sell it to me. When he asked me what I wanted it for I told him that it was to summon people to prayer, whereupon he offered to show me a better way: it was to say thrice 'God is great! I bear witness that there is no god but God, I bear witness that Muḥammad is the Messenger of Allah. Come to prayer. Come to prayer. Come to success. Come to success. God is great, God is great. There is no god but God.'" When the Prophet was told of this he said that it was a true vision if God so willed it, and that he should go with Bilāl and communicate it to him so that he might call to prayer, for he had a sweeter and more penetrating voice. When Bilāl acted as *mu'adhdhin* 'Umar heard him in his house and came to the Prophet dragging his cloak on the ground and saying that he had seen precisely the same vision. The Prophet said, "God be praised for that!"[15]

The Battle of Badr

Ibn Isḥāq reports that 'Abd Raḥmān ibn 'Awf said about Umayyah as he was leading him and his son away as his captive after the fighting at Badr:

> Umayyah said to me as I walked between them holding their hands, "Who is that man who is wearing an ostrich feather

[15] Abū Dāwūd, Ibn Mājah, Aḥmad and As-Suyūṭī, 2004, p. 80; Ibn Isḥāq, 2007, pp. 235-236.

> on his breast?" When I told him it was Ḥamzah he said that it was he who had done them so much damage. As I was leading them away Bilāl saw him with me. It was Umayyah who used to torture Bilāl in Makkah to make him abandon Islam, bringing him out to the scorching heat of the sun, laying him on his back, and putting a great stone on his chest, telling him that he could stay there until he gave up the religion of Muḥammad, and Bilāl kept saying "One! One!" As soon as he saw him he said, "The arch-infidel Umayyah ibn Khalaf! May I not live if he lives." I said, "Would you attack my prisoners?" But he kept crying out these words in spite of my remonstrances until finally he shouted at the top of his voice, "O God's Helpers, the arch-infidel Umayyah ibn Khalaf is here! May I not live if he lives." The people formed a ring round us as I was protecting him. Then a man drew his sword and cut off his son's foot so that he fell down and Umayyah let out a cry such as I have never heard; and I said to him, "Make your escape (though he had no chance of escape), I can do nothing for you." They hewed them to pieces with their swords until they were dead. 'Abd Raḥmān used to say, "God have mercy on Bilāl. I lost my coats of mail and he deprived me of my prisoners."[16]

His Relationship with the Prophet ﷺ

Bilāl was the confidant of the Prophet ﷺ, his treasurer and *mu'adhdhin.* Ibn Isḥāq reports:

> When the Prophet left Khaybar and was on the way, he said towards the end of the night, "Who will watch over us till dawn so that we may sleep?" Bilāl volunteered to do so, so he laid down and slept. Bilāl got up and prayed as long as God willed that he should; then he propped himself against

[16] Ibn Isḥāq, 2007, p. 303.

> his camel, and there was the dawn as he was looking at it, and his eyes were heavy and he slept. The first thing to wake the others was the feel of the sun. The Prophet was the first to wake up and he asked Bilāl what he had done to them. He said that the same thing had happened to him as had happened to the Prophet, and he admitted that he was right. Then the Prophet let himself be taken a short distance; then he made his camel kneel, and he and the men performed their ablutions. Then he ordered Bilāl to call to prayer, and the Prophet led them in prayer.[17]

Ibn al-Mubārak reported in *al-Birr wa'ṣ-Ṣilah,* and Al-Bukhārī and Muslim cited part of the hadith, that Abū Dharr was embroiled in a heated argument with Bilāl. Carried away by his anger, Abū Dharr said to Bilāl, "You son of a black woman!" Bilāl complained about this to the Prophet ﷺ, who turned to Abū Dharr, rebuking him, "You have exceeded the limit, Abū Dharr! You are a man that still has traces of *Jāhiliyyah* (pre-Islamic days of Ignorance) in you. Do you not know that there is no difference between an Arab and a non-Arab except by *taqwā* (piety)?" Upon hearing this Abū Dharr immediately placed his head on the ground and urged Bilāl to put his foot on Abū Dharr's face in the ground. Instead Bilāl forgave his brother in faith and took him by the hand.[18]

Al-Qurṭubī relates in his Qur'ānic exegesis the following story: Bilāl proposed marriage to the daughter of Al-Bakīr, but her brothers refused. Bilāl said, "Messenger of Allah ﷺ! What is wrong with the

---

[17] Ibn Isḥāq, 2007, p. 517.

[18] Ibn Taymiyyah, 2003, p. 67 and Al-Qaraḍāwī, 2003, p. 229. Al-Bukhārī and Muslim have a part of the story without explicit mention of Bilāl or the reference to his mother being black. Al-Bukhārī, *kitāb al-īmān, bāb al-ma'āṣī min amr al-jāhilīyyah wa lā yakfuru ṣāḥibuhā bi'rtikābihā illā bi'sh-shirk,* No. 30, and *kitāb al-'itq, bāb qawl an-Nabiyyi, ṣalla'llāhu 'alayhi wa sallama, al-'abīdu ikhwānukum fa aṭ'imūhum mimmā ta'kulūn,* No. 2407; Muslim, *al-aymān wa'n-nudhūr, bāb iṭ'ām al-mamlūk mimmā ya'kulu wa ilbāsuhu mimmā yalbisu wa lā yukallifuhu mā yaghlibuh,* No. 1661.

sons of Al-Bakīr? I asked for their sister's hand in marriage and they refused me and caused me injury." The Messenger of Allah ﷺ became angry for the sake of Bilāl. The news of that reached them and they went to their sister and said, "What trouble we have endured because of you!" Their sister said, "My affair is in the hand of the Messenger of Allah ﷺ." So they married her to Bilāl.[19]

Abū Ruwayḥah Khālid al-Khath'amī

Ibn Isḥāq reports:

> Bilāl, the *mawlā* (freed slave) of Abū Bakr and the *mu'adhdhin* of the Messenger of Allah ﷺ and Abū Ruwayḥah 'Abdullāh ibn 'Abd ar-Raḥmān, who was al-Khath'amī and one of al-Faza', were brothers. ... When 'Umar ibn al-Khaṭṭāb compiled the registers in Syria, and Bilāl had gone there and remained as a *mujāhid* (combatant), 'Umar said to Bilāl, "With whom do you wish to be grouped in the *dīwān* register, Bilāl?" and he said, "With Abū Ruwayḥah. I will never leave him, because of the brotherhood the Messenger of Allah ﷺ established between us." So he was linked with him and the register of the Abyssinians was linked with Khath'am because of Bilāl's position with them, and it is with Khath'am to this day in Syria.[20]

Ibn Sa'd reported that Bilāl interceded for Abū Ruwayḥah to marry an Arab woman from a prominent family.

Life after the Prophet ﷺ

When the Prophet ﷺ passed away, Bilāl was asked to make the *adhān* in the mosque of the Prophet ﷺ who had not even been buried yet. When Bilāl ؓ reached the line of the *adhān*, 'I bear witness that Muḥammad

---

[19] Al-Qurṭubī, 2009, vol. 3, p. 468.
[20] Ibn Isḥāq, 2007, p. 235.

is the Messenger of Allah ﷺ,' everyone in the mosque wept. After the Messenger of Allah ﷺ was buried, Abū Bakr ﷺ asked Bilāl to make the *adhān* again. Bilāl replied, "If you freed me so that I would be under your service then you have the right to order me that. But if you freed me for the sake of Allah, then leave me to make my own decision." Abū Bakr ﷺ replied, "I only freed you for the sake of Allah." "If that is the case, I will not make the *adhān* for anyone after the Prophet ﷺ," said Bilāl. Abū Bakr ﷺ responded, "As you wish." Bilāl stayed in Madīnah for a while, then he went to Abū Bakr ﷺ and said, "Caliph of the Messenger of Allah ﷺ! I heard the Messenger of Allah ﷺ say, 'The best deed for the believer is *jihād* in the way of Allah." Abū Bakr ﷺ pleaded for Bilāl to stay with him in Madīnah, but Bilāl wanted to go and join the *mujāhidun* in Sham. When the Muslims conquered Jerusalem, 'Umar ibn al-Khaṭṭāb ﷺ asked Bilāl to make the *adhān* one last time. 'Umar said to Bilāl, "Abū Bakr is our master and he freed our master (meaning Bilāl)." When Bilāl made the *adhān*, everyone wept. Bilāl died in Damascus when he was just over sixty years old.[21]

Aṣḥam ibn Abjar an-Najashī (The Negus)

Aṣḥam an-Najashī (the Negus) was the King of Abyssinia at the time of the Prophet ﷺ. Formerly a Christian, the Negus was a just and righteous ruler. When the Messenger of Allah ﷺ saw the affliction of his Companions by the Makkan idolators, he said to them, "If you were to go to Abyssinia (it would be better for you), for the king (i.e. the Negus) will not tolerate injustice and it is a friendly country, until such a time as Allah shall relieve you from your distress."[22] The Negus allowed the Muslims to stay in his land despite the protests of the Makkans. He is reported to be the only person to receive the honour of having the Prophet ﷺ pray the funeral prayer for him whilst he was in a different land.

---

21 As-Suyūṭī, 2004, p. 83.
22 Ibn Isḥāq, 2007, p. 146.

His Name

As-Suyūṭī reports, "The word *an-Najāshī* (the Negus) is an Abyssinian word. Imam aṭ-Ṭabarī, the dean of Qur'ānic exegesis, said that *an-Najāshī* is an Arabic word from the word *najash*, meaning a sign or increase. He also said that the word (*an-Najāshī*) is a title used for an Abyssinian king, similar to the way that the Muslim Caliph is called *Amīr al-Mu'minīn*, 'Leader of the Believers' and as Caesar is used by the Romans, Khan by the Turks, Emperor by the Persians and Pharaoh by the Ancient Egyptians."[23] Ibn Isḥāq said, "The name of the Negus was Aṣḥam which is 'Aṭiyyah in Arabic."[24]

How the Negus Became King of Abyssinia

Ibn Isḥāq reported that 'Urwah ibn az-Zubayr said to az-Zuhrī, "Do you know what the Negus meant when he said that God took no bribe from me when He gave me back my kingdom that I should take a bribe for it, and God did not do what men wanted against me so why should I do what they want against Him?" When I [az-Zuhrī] said that I did not know, he said that 'Ā'ishah ﵂ told him that the father of the Negus was the king, and the Negus was his only son. The Negus had an uncle who had twelve sons who were of the Abyssinian royal house. The Abyssinians said among themselves, "It would be a good thing if we were to kill the father of the Negus and make his brother king, because he has no son but this youngster, while his brother has twelve sons, so they can inherit the kingdom after him so that the future of Abyssinia may be permanently secured." So they attacked the Negus's father and killed him, making his brother king, and such was the state of affairs for a considerable time.

The Negus grew up with his uncle, an intelligent and resolute young man. He attained an ascendancy over his uncle to such a degree that

---

[23] As-Suyūṭī, 2004, p. 61.

[24] Ibn al-Jawzī, 1998, p. 104.

when the Abyssinians perceived how great his influence with the king was, they began to fear lest he might gain the crown, and would then put them all to death because he knew that they were the murderers of his father. Accordingly they went to his uncle and said, "Either you must kill this young man or you must exile him from among us, for we are in fear of our lives because of him." He replied, "You wretches, but yesterday I slew his father, and am I to kill him today? But I will put him out of your country." So they took him to the market and sold him to a merchant for six hundred dirhams. The latter threw him into a boat and went off with him, but on that very evening the autumn storm clouds massed, and his uncle went out to pray for rain beneath the mass of cloud when he was struck by lightning and killed. The Abyssinians hastened in fear to his sons, and lo! he was a begetter of fools; he had not a son who was any good at all; the situation of the Abyssinians became unsettled, and when they feared the pressure of events they said to one another, "Know, by God, that your king, the only one who can put us to rights, is the one you sold this morning, and if you care about your country go after him now." So they went out in search of him and the man to whom they had sold him, until they overtook him and took the Negus from him. They then brought him home, put the crown on his head, made him sit upon the throne, and proclaimed him king.

The merchant to whom they had sold him came and said, "Either you give me my money or I shall tell him about this." They said, "We will not give you a penny." He said, "In that case, by God, I will speak to him." They said, "Well, there he is"; so he came and stood before him and said, "O King, I bought a young slave from people in the market for six hundred dirhams. They gave me my slave and they took my money, yet when I had gone off with my slave they overtook me and seized my slave and kept my money." The Negus said, "You must either give him his money back or let the young man place his hand in his, and let him take him where he wishes." They replied, "No, but we will give him his money." For this reason he said the words in question. This was the first thing that was reported about his firmness in his religion and his justice in judgement.[25]

The Abyssinians Revolt Against the Negus

When Quraysh saw that the Companions of the Prophet ﷺ were safely ensconced in Abyssinia and had found security there, they decided to send two determined men to the Negus to get them sent back, so that they could get them out of the land in which they were living in peace and seduce them from their religion. So they sent 'Abdullāh ibn Abī Rabī'ah and 'Amr ibn al-'Āṣ. They collected some presents to take to the Negus and his generals. When Abū Ṭālib perceived their design he composed the following verse to move the Negus to treat the Muslims kindly and protect them:

> Would that I knew how far away Ja'far and 'Amr fare,
> (The bitterest enemies are oft the nearest in blood).
> Does the Negus still treat Ja'far and his companions kindly,
> Or has the mischief-maker prevented him?
> You are noble and generous, may you escape calamity;
> No refugees are unhappy with you.
> Know that Allah has increased your happiness
> And all prosperity cleaves to you.
> You are a river whose banks overflow with bounty
> Which reaches both friend and foe.

Umm Salamah ﵂, the wife of the Prophet ﷺ, said, "When we reached Abyssinia the Negus gave us a kind reception. We safely practised our religion, and we worshipped God, and suffered no wrong in word or

---

[25] Ibn Isḥāq, 2007, pp. 153-154.

deed. When the Quraysh got to know of that, they decided to send two determined men to the Negus and to give him presents of the choicest wares of Makkah. Leatherwork was especially prized there, so they collected a great many skins so that they were able to give some to every one of his generals. They sent 'Abdullāh and 'Amr with instructions to give each general his present before they spoke to the Negus about the refugees. Then they were to give their presents to the Negus and ask him to give the men up before he spoke to them. They carried out these instructions to the letter and said to each of the generals, 'Some foolish fellows from our people have taken refuge in the king's country. They have forsaken our religion and not accepted yours, but have brought in an invented religion which neither we nor you know anything about. Our nobles have sent us to the king to get him to return them, so when we speak to the king about them, advise him to surrender them to us and not to speak to them, for their own people have the keenest insight and know most about their faults.' This, the generals agreed to do. They took their gifts to the Negus and when he had accepted them, they said to him what they had already said to the generals about the refugees. Now there was nothing which 'Abdullāh and 'Amr disliked more than that the Negus should hear what the Muslims had to say. The generals about his presence said that the men had spoken truly, and their own people best knew the truth about the refugees, and they recommended the king to give them up and return them to their own people. The Negus was enraged and said, 'No, by God, I will not surrender them. No people who have sought my permission, settled in my country, and chosen me rather than others shall be betrayed, until I summon them and ask them about what these two men allege. If they are as they say, I will give them up to them and send them back to their own people; but if what they say is false, I will protect them and see that they receive proper hospitality while under my protection.'

Then he summoned the Companions of the Prophet ﷺ, and when his messenger came they gathered together, saying one to another, 'What will you say to the man when you come to him?' They said, 'We shall say what we know and what our Prophet ﷺ commanded us, come what may.' When they came into the royal presence they found that the king had summoned his bishops with their sacred books exposed around him. He asked them what was the religion for which they had forsaken their people, without entering into his religion or any other. Ja'far ibn Abū Ṭālib answered, 'O King, we were an uncivilised people, worshipping idols, eating corpses, committing abominations, breaking natural ties, treating guests badly, and our strong devoured our weak. Thus we were until God sent us a Prophet whose lineage, truth, trustworthiness, and clemency we know. He summoned us to acknowledge God's unity and to worship him and to renounce the stones and images which we and our fathers formerly worshipped. He commanded us to speak the truth, be faithful to our engagements, mindful of the ties of kinship and kindly hospitality, and to refrain from crimes and bloodshed. He forbade us to commit abominations and to speak lies, and to devour the property of orphans, to vilify chaste women. He commanded us to worship God alone and not to associate anything with Him, and he gave us orders about prayer, almsgiving, and fasting (enumerating the commands of Islam). We confessed his truth and believed in him, and we followed him in what he had brought from God, and we worshipped God alone without associating aught with Him. We treated as forbidden what he forbade, and as lawful what he declared lawful. Thereupon our people attacked us, treated us harshly and seduced us from our faith to try to make us go back to the worship of idols instead of the worship of God, and to regard as lawful the evil deeds we once committed. So when they got the better of us, treated us unjustly and circumscribed our lives, and came between us and our religion, we came to your country, having chosen you above all others. Here we have been happy in your protection, and we hope that we shall not be treated unjustly while we are with you, O King.'

The Negus asked if they had with them anything which had come from God. When Ja'far said that he had, the Negus commanded him to read it to him, so he read him a passage from Sūrah Maryam. The Negus wept until his beard was wet and the bishops wept until their scrolls were wet, when they heard what he read to them. Then the Negus said, 'Of a truth, this and what Jesus brought have come from the same niche. You two may go, for by God, I will never give them up to them and they shall not be betrayed.'

When the two had gone, 'Amr said, 'Tomorrow I will tell him something that will uproot them all.' 'Abdullāh, who was the more God-fearing of them in his attitude towards us, said, 'Do not do it, for they are our kindred though they have gone against us.' He said, 'By God, I will tell him that they assert that Jesus, son of Mary, is a creature.' He went to him in the morning and told him that they said a dreadful thing about Jesus, son of Mary, and that he should send for them and ask them about it. He did so. Nothing of the kind had happened to them before, and the people gathered together asking one another what they should say about Jesus when they were asked. They decided that they would say what God had said and what the Prophet had brought, come what may. So when they went into the royal presence and the question was put to them, Ja'far answered, 'We say about him that which our Prophet brought, saying, he is the slave of God, and His Prophet, and His spirit, and His word, which he cast into Mary the blessed virgin.' The Negus took a stick from the ground and said, 'By God, Jesus, son of Mary, does not exceed what you have said by the length of this stick.' His generals around about him snorted when he said this, and he said, 'Though you snort, by God! Go, for you are safe in my country.' Then he repeated three times the words, 'He who curses you will be fined. Not for a mountain of gold would I allow a man of you to be hurt.' 'Give them back their presents, for I have no use for them. God took no bribe from me when He gave me back my kingdom, that I should take a bribe for it, and God did not do what men wanted against me, so why should I do what they want against Him.' So they left his presence, crestfallen, taking away their rejected gifts, while we lived with him comfortably in the best security.

While we were living thus, a rebel arose to snatch his kingdom from him, and I never knew us to be so sad as we were at that, in our anxiety lest this would get the better of the Negus, and that a man would arise who did not know our case as the Negus did. He went out against him, and the Nile lay between the two parties. The Prophet's Companions called for a man who would go to the battle and bring back news, and Az-Zubayr ibn al-Awwām volunteered. Now he was the youngest man we had. We inflated a waterskin and he put it under his chest, and swam across until he reached that point of the Nile where the armies faced one another. Then he went on until he met them. Meanwhile we prayed to God to give the Negus victory over his enemy and to establish him in his own country; and as we were doing so, waiting for what might happen, up came Az-Zubayr running, waving his clothes as he said, 'Hurrah, the Negus has conquered and God has destroyed his enemies and established him in his land.' By God, I never knew us to be so happy before. The Negus came back, God having destroyed his enemy and established him in his country, and the chiefs of the Abyssinians rallied to him. Meanwhile we lived in the happiest conditions until we came to the Apostle of God ﷺ in Makkah."[26]

Correspondence with the Prophet ﷺ

The Prophet ﷺ sent 'Amr ibn Umayyah aḍ-Ḍamrī to the Negus about Ja'far ibn Abī Ṭālib and his companions and sent a letter with him: "From Muḥammad, the Messenger of Allah, to the Negus al-Aṣḥam king of Abyssinia, Peace. I praise God unto you, the King, the Holy,

[26] Ibn Isḥāq, 2007, pp. 150-153.

the Peace, the Faithful, the Watcher, and I bear witness that Jesus, son of Mary, is the Spirit of God and His word, which He cast to Mary the Virgin, the good, the pure, so that she conceived Jesus. God created him from His spirit and His breathing as He created Adam by His hand and His breathing. I call you to God, the Unique without partner, and to His obedience, and to follow me and believe in that which came to me, for I am the Messenger of Allah. I have sent to you my cousin Ja'far with a number of Muslims, and when they come to you entertain them without haughtiness, for I invite you and your armies to God. I have accomplished my work and my admonition, so receive my advice. Peace upon all those that follow true guidance."

The Negus replied, "From the Negus al-Aṣḥam ibn Abjar, peace upon you, O Prophet of God, and mercy and blessings from God beside whom there is no god, who has guided me to Islam. I have received your letter in which you mention the matter of Jesus and by the Lord of heaven and earth he is not a scrap more than what you say. We know that with which you were sent to us and we have entertained your cousin and his companions. I testify that you are God's Messenger, true and confirming (those before you). I have given my fealty to you and to your cousin and I have surrendered myself through him to the Lord of the worlds. I have sent to you my son, Arhā. I have control over myself and if you wish me to come to you, O Messenger of Allah ﷺ, I will do so. I bear witness that what you say is true."[27]

Marriage Between Umm Ḥabībah and the Prophet ﷺ

A few months before Ḥudaybiyah, news had come from Abyssinia of the death of 'Ubaydullāh ibn Jashsh, the Prophet's cousin and brother-in-law. He had been a Christian before he entered Islam, and not long after his emigration to Abyssinia he had reverted to Christianity. This had greatly distressed his wife Umm Ḥabībah, Abū Sufyān's daughter,

[27] Ibn Isḥāq, 2007, pp. 657-658.

who remained a Muslim; and when four months elapsed after the death of her husband the Prophet sent a message to the Negus, asking him to stand proxy for himself and to ratify a marriage between him and the widow, if she were willing. To her the Prophet ﷺ sent no message directly; but she had a dream in which someone came to her and addressed her as 'Mother of the Believers',[28] and she interpreted this as meaning that she would become the wife of the Prophet ﷺ. The next day she received the message from the Negus which confirmed her dream, whereupon she chose her kinsman Khālid ibn Sa'īd to give her in marriage, and he and the Negus solemnised the pact between them in the presence of Ja'far and others of the brethren. Then the Negus held a wedding feast in his palace, and all the Muslims were invited.[29]

His Death

At the beginning of the Islamic month of Rajab, word of the death of the Negus came to the Prophet ﷺ. After the next ritual prayer to be prayed in the mosque, he turned to the congregation and said, "This day a righteous slave of Allah, Aṣḥam, has died. And he stood and led us as imām and prayed over him."[30] Then he led them in the funeral prayer after proclaiming "Allahu Akbar! (Allah is Great!)" four times.[31] 'Ā'ishah ﷺ said, "When the Negus died, it used to be said that a light was constantly seen over his grave."[32]

---

[28] The 'Mother of the Believers' is an honorific title given to the wives of the Prophet ﷺ. The title is derived from the Qur'ānic verse, "*The Prophet is closer to the Believers than their own selves, and his wives are their mothers.*" Sūrat al-Aḥzāb 33:6.

[29] Lings, 1983, p. 259.

[30] Muslim, *kitāb al-janā'iz, bāb fī at-takbīrāt*, No. 952, see also Nos. 951 and 953. Al-Bukhārī, *kitāb faḍā'il aṣ-ṣaḥābah, bāb mawt an-Najāshī*, No. 3664; Ahmad, As-Suyūṭī, 2004, p. 66. The wording is that of Muslim.

[31] Muslim, *kitāb al-janā'iz, bāb fī at-takbīrāt*, No. 952; Al-Bukhārī, *kitāb faḍā'il aṣ-ṣaḥābah, bāb mawt an-Najāshī*, No. 3664.

[32] Ibn Isḥāq, 2007, p. 154.

Usāmah ibn Zayd ibn Ḥārithah

Usāmah was the son of Zayd ibn Ḥārithah, the former adopted son of the Prophet ﷺ, and Umm Ayman, the wet-nurse of the Prophet ﷺ. Resembling his African mother, Usāmah was dark in complexion with a broad nose. Some of the hypocrites in Madīnah spread a rumour that Usāmah was not the son of Zayd because Zayd was very fair in complexion. 'Ā'ishah ﵂ said, "A *qā'if* (one skilled in recognising the lineage of a person through physiognomy) came to see me while the Prophet ﷺ was present, and Usāmah ibn Zayd and Zayd ibn Ḥārithah were lying asleep. He said, 'These feet (of Usāmah and his father) are of persons belonging to each other.'" The Prophet ﷺ was pleased with that, and informed 'Ā'ishah ﵂ about it.[33] Usāmah was a similar age to Al-Ḥasan ibn 'Alī ibn Abī Ṭālib, the grandson of the Prophet ﷺ. The Prophet ﷺ treated Usāmah as if he was his grandson. When Usāmah was informed that he would not be allowed to fight in the Battle of Uḥud, due to his youth, his eyes flowed with tears. However, Usāmah was permitted to fight in the Battle of the Ditch when he was fifteen years old. He fought valiantly and held firm in the Battle of Ḥunayn, protecting the Prophet ﷺ. In the Battle of Mu'tah, Usāmah fought under the banner of his father, Zayd ibn Ḥārithah. Usāmah witnessed the death of his father at this battle, when he was just eighteen years old. Usāmah was not yet twenty years old, when the Prophet ﷺ instructed him to lead the Muslim army consisting of senior and prominent Companions such as Abū Bakr, 'Umar and Sa'd ibn Abī Waqqās ﵃. The battle was against the Byzantine Greeks. So beloved was Usāmah to the Prophet ﷺ, that when some of the people criticised Usāmah's appointment as leader, the Prophet ﷺ said, "If you are criticising Usāmah's leadership, you used to criticise his father's

---

33 Al-Bukhārī, *kitāb faḍā'il aṣ-ṣaḥābah, manāqib Zayd ibn Ḥārithah, mawlā'n-Nabiyyi, ṣalla'llāhu 'alayhi wa sallama*, No. 3525.

leadership before. By Allah! He was worthy of leadership and was one of the most beloved persons to me, and now Usāmah is the most beloved person to me after Zayd."[34]

A female Companion went to the Prophet ﷺ seeking his advice. Two men had already proposed to her and she wanted his advice on whom to marry. The Prophet ﷺ told her not to marry either of the two, as one of them was known to be harsh with his womenfolk whilst the other would not be able to provide for his wife. The Prophet ﷺ recommended her to marry Usāmah ibn Zayd. The woman refused as she did not like Usāmah. The Prophet ﷺ insisted that she should marry Usāmah which she subsequently did. Allah blessed their marriage with goodness and the woman was very happy with Usāmah.[35] 'Umar ﷺ, the second caliph, used to honour Usāmah and prefer him over his own son because of the love of the Prophet ﷺ for him. Usāmah refrained from participating in the civil war between 'Alī and Mu'āwiyah ﷺ. He died towards the end of the reign of Mu'āwiyah in the fifty-fourth year of the *hijrah*.[36]

Waḥshī ibn Ḥarb

Waḥshī ibn Ḥarb was an Abyssinian Companion of the Prophet ﷺ, best known, prior to accepting Islam, for killing the leader of the martyrs, Ḥamzah ibn 'Abd al-Muṭṭalib, the uncle of the Messenger of Allah ﷺ. Afterwards he killed Musaylimah the Liar. Waḥshī also participated in

---

[34] Al-Bukhārī, *kitāb faḍā'il aṣ-ṣaḥābah, manāqib Zayd ibn Ḥārithah, mawlā'n-Nabiyyi, ṣalla'llāhu 'alayhi wa sallama*, No. 3524; Muslim, *faḍā'il aṣ-ṣaḥābah, bāb faḍā'il Zayd ibn Ḥārithah wa Usāmah ibn Zayd, raḍiya'llāhu 'anhumā*, No. 2426.

[35] Muslim, *kitāb aṭ-ṭalāq, bāb al-muṭallaqah thalāthan lā nafaqata lahā*, No. 1480; Ibn Ḥibbān, *dhikr al-khabar ad-dālli 'alā anna hadha'z-zajar innamā zajarun idhā rakana aḥadumā ilā ṣāḥibihi wa huwa'l-'illata'llatī dhakarnāhā*, No. 4049; Ibn al-Jawzī, 1998, pp. 131-133.

[36] Ibn Ḥajar, 2008, in commentary on hadith No. 3523 of *Ṣaḥīḥ al-Bukhārī* in *Fatḥ al-Bārī*.

the Battle of Yarmūk. He resided and died in Ḥimṣ and lived until the caliphate of 'Uthmān ⁂.³⁷

Killing Ḥamzah

Ibn Isḥāq reports:

> Jubayr ibn Muṭ'im summoned an Abyssinian slave of his called Waḥshī, who could throw a javelin as the Abyssinians do and seldom missed the mark. He said "Go forth with the army, and if you kill Ḥamzah, Muḥammad's uncle, in revenge for my uncle, Ṭu'aymah ibn 'Adī, you shall be free." So Quraysh marched forth with the flower of their army, and their black troops, and their adherents from the tribe of Kinānah, and the people of the lowland, and women in howdahs went with them to stir up their anger and prevent their running away. Whenever Hind passed Waḥshī or he passed by her, she would say, "Come on, you father of blackness, satisfy your vengeance and ours." Waḥshī had the title of Abū Dasmah.³⁸

Ibn Isḥāq reports from Ja'far ibn 'Amr ibn Umayyah aḍ-Ḍamrī: "I went out with 'Ubaydullāh ibn 'Adī ibn al-Khiyār, brother of the people of Nawfal ibn 'Abd al-Manāf in the time of Mu'āwiyah ibn Abī Sufyān and we made an excursion with the army. When we came back we passed by Ḥimṣ where Waḥshī had taken his abode. When we arrived there 'Ubaydullāh said to me, "Shall we go and see Waḥshī and ask him how he killed Ḥamzah?" "If you like," I said. So we went to inquire about him in Ḥimṣ. While we were doing so a man said to us, "You will find him in the courtyard of his house. He is a man much addicted to

---

³⁷   Ibn Ḥajar.
³⁷   Ibn Ḥajar.
³⁸   Ibn Isḥāq, 2007, p. 371.

wine; and if you find him sober, you will find an Arab and will get what you want from him in answer to your questions; but if you find him in his usual state, then leave him alone." So we walked off to find him, and there he was in the courtyard of his house upon a carpet, an old man like a bird (*bughāth*). He was quite sober and normal. We saluted him, and he lifted his head to look at 'Ubaydullāh, and said, "Are you the son of 'Adī ibn al-Khiyār?" and when he said he was, he said, "By God, I have not seen you since I handed you to your Sa'dite mother who nursed you in Dhū Ṭuwā. I handed you to her when she was on her camel, and she clasped you round your body with her two hands. You kicked me with your feet when I lifted you up to her. By God, as soon as you stood in front of me I recognised them." We sat down and told him that we had come to hear his account of how he killed Ḥamzah. He said, "I will tell you as I told the Prophet ﷺ when he asked me about it. I was a slave of Jubayr ibn Muṭ'im, whose uncle Ṭu'aymah ibn 'Adī had been killed at Badr, and when Quraysh set out for Uḥud, Jubayr told me that if I killed Ḥamzah, Muhammad's uncle, in revenge for his uncle, I should be free. So I went out with the army, a young Abyssinian, skilful like my countrymen in the use of the javelin – I hardly ever missed anything with it. When the fight began I went out to look carefully for Ḥamzah, until I saw him in the midst of the army, like a great camel, slaying men with his sword, none being able to resist him, and by God, I was getting ready for him, making towards him and hiding myself behind trees or rocks so that he might come near me, when suddenly Sibā' got to him first, and when Ḥamzah saw him, he said, 'Come here, you son of a female circumciser,' and struck him a blow so swiftly that it seemed to miss his head. I poised my javelin until I was sure that it would hit the mark and launched it at him. It pierced the lower part of his body and came out between his legs, and he began to stagger towards me. Then he collapsed, and I left him with the javelin until he died; then I came back and recovered my javelin, and returned to the camp and stayed there, for I had no further business, and my only object in killing him was that I might be freed. When I returned to Makkah I was freed and lived there until the Prophet ﷺ conquered Makkah, when I fled to Ṭā'if, and stayed there for some time. When the envoys of Ṭā'if went out to the Prophet ﷺ to surrender, I was in an impasse and thought that I would go to Syria or the Yemen, or any other country, and while I was in this anxiety a man said to me, 'Good heavens, what is the matter? He does not kill anyone who enters his religion and pronounces the *shahādah.*' On hearing this I went out of town to the Prophet ﷺ at Madīnah, and the first thing to surprise him was to see me standing at his head, witnessing to the truth of God and His Messenger. When he saw me he said, 'Is this Waḥshī?' 'Yes, O Messenger of Allah ﷺ,' I said. He replied, 'Sit down and tell me how you killed Ḥamzah.' So I told him as I have told you. When I had finished he said, 'Woe to you, hide your face from me and never let me see you again.' So I used to avoid the Prophet ﷺ wherever he was so that he should not see me, until God took him."[39]

Ibn Isḥāq reports in another narration: When Waḥshī went to Madīnah the men said, "O Prophet, this is Waḥshī" to which he replied, "Leave him alone, for that one man should accept Islam is dearer to me than the killing of a thousand unbelievers."[40]

Killing Musaylimah

Waḥshī said: "When the Muslims went out against Musaylimah, the false prophet, lord of the Yamāmah, I accompanied them, and I took the javelin with which I had killed Ḥamzah, and when the armies met I saw Musaylimah standing with a sword in his hand, but I did not recognise him. I made ready for him and so did one of the *Anṣār* from the other side, both of us intending to kill him. I poised my javelin until I was sure that it would hit the mark, and launched it at him, and it pierced him, and the *Anṣārī* rushed at him and smote him with his

---

[39] Ibn Isḥāq, 2007, pp. 375-376.

[40] Ibn Isḥāq, 2007, p. 377.

sword, so your Lord knows best which of us killed him. If I killed him, then I killed the best man after the Prophet ﷺ and I have also killed the worst man."[41]

Sa'd al-Aswad

Ibn al-Jawzī narrates on the authority of Mālik: A man went to the Messenger of Allah ﷺ and said, "Does the blackness of my skin and wretchedness of my form prevent me from entering the Garden?" The Prophet ﷺ replied, "Definitely not! By the One Who has my soul in His Hand, the one who has *taqwā* of Allah and believes in what His Messenger brought will gain admission to the Garden." Sa'd said to the Prophet ﷺ, "I swear by the One Who honoured you with prophethood. I bear witness that there is no god but Allah alone without partner and I bear witness that Muḥammad is His slave and Messenger. So what do I have, O Messenger of Allah?" "You have the same rights and obligations in the religion as the Muslim community. You are now a brother to them," the Prophet ﷺ replied. The man then said, "I asked many people who are gathered here with you and others who are not here for a woman in marriage. They all rejected my proposal due to the blackness of my skin and the wretchedness of my face. I am a man of standing from amongst my own people from the tribe of Sālim; our ancestors are renowned. But unfortunately I inherited dark skin from my maternal uncles." The Messenger of Allah ﷺ asked the congregation, "Have you seen 'Amr ibn Wuhayb today?"' The people replied, "No we have not." The Messenger ﷺ asked them, "Does anyone know where he lives?" Someone said he did. The Messenger then ordered Sa'd, "Go to his house and lightly knock on his door. Then convey greetings to him. If he allows you to enter his house say to him: 'The Messenger of Allah ﷺ has married me to one of your daughters.'" 'Amr ibn Wuhayb had a daughter who was beautiful and

---

41 Ibn Isḥāq, 2007, p. 377; As-Suyūṭī, 2004, pp. 92-93.

very intelligent. When Sa‘d knocked and conveyed his greetings to the people of the household, they hospitably welcomed him after hearing his eloquent use of the Arabic language. After they opened the door and saw the blackness of his skin and the wretchedness of his face they were abhorrent. Sa‘d said, “The Messenger of Allah ﷺ has married me to one of your daughters.” The family vigorously rejected his proposal. As Sa‘d was leaving the house a woman appeared from her chamber saying, “Come back, slave of Allah. If the Messenger of Allah ﷺ has married me to you then I am pleased with whatever Allah and His Messenger are pleased with for me.” Sa‘d returned to the Messenger of Allah ﷺ and informed him about what occurred. The woman said to her father, “Father, remember your salvation, your salvation, before the revelation disgraces you. If the Messenger of Allah ﷺ has married me to him then I am definitely pleased with what pleases the Messenger of Allah ﷺ.” Her father left in search of the Messenger of Allah ﷺ. He found him at the back of the congregation. Upon seeing him, the Prophet ﷺ asked him, “Are you the one who rejected the ruling of the Messenger of Allah?” The father said: “Indeed I am him, I seek forgiveness from Allah. I thought that he (Sa‘d) was lying. I hereby marry my daughter to him. We seek refuge in Allah from His wrath and the wrath of His Messenger.” “Go to your son-in-law and introduce him to her,” said the Prophet ﷺ. “I swear by the One Who sent you with the truth I will not take anything (regarding her dowry) until I consult my brothers,” the man said. The Messenger ﷺ responded, “The dowry of your daughter is with three men amongst the believers. Go to ‘Uthmān ibn ‘Affān and take a hundred dirhams from him.” The man went and ‘Uthmān gave him even more than the prescribed amount. “Go to ‘Alī ibn Abī Ṭālib and take a hundred dirhams from him.” ‘Alī also gave the man more than the prescribed amount. “And go to ‘Abd ar-Raḥmān ibn ‘Awf and take a hundred dirhams from him.” ‘Abd ar-Raḥmān did the same as ‘Uthmān and ‘Alī رضي الله عنهم by giving him more than he expected.

When Sa'd was in the market looking for what to buy for his new marital home he heard a voice calling, "O cavalry of Allah, mount your horses and I convey to you glad tidings." Sa'd cast his gaze at the skies and said, "O Allah, Lord of the heavens and the earth, Lord of Muḥammad. Today I solemnly vow that I will make use of these dirhams for what pleases Allah, His Messenger and the believers." Sa'd promptly jumped to his feet and dashed to mount a highborn horse. He purchased a sword, lance and horse as well as a long outer garment. He fastened one turban around his waist and covered his face with another turban. Nothing could be seen of him except his two eyes. When Sa'd joined the *Muhājirūn* (Emigrants) in the army ranks, they inquired amongst themselves, "Who is this horseman whom we do not recognise?" Even the Messenger of Allah ﷺ was curious about this mysterious horseman, "Who is this horseman who has not come to greet us?"

Soon thereafter the battle commenced, the two squadrons plunged against one another. Sa'd threw himself into the midst of the battle, began to strike the enemy with his sword, and thrust his lance into everyone he faced. Suddenly one of the enemy's horsemen attacked Sa'd and uncovered his arms. When the Messenger of Allah ﷺ saw the blackness of the arms of this brave soldier, he recognised him. "Is it you Sa'd?" he asked. Sa'd replied, "May my mother and my father be your ransom, Messenger of Allah ﷺ." The Messenger said, "Sa'd, you have striven earnestly for Allah and His *dīn*." Sa'd continued to fight, striking with his sword and thrusting his lance into the enemy. Then the Muslims called out, "Sa'd has been struck down!" Upon hearing this, the Messenger of Allah ﷺ went towards his fallen Companion. Upon approaching Sa'd, the Prophet ﷺ raised Sa'd's head and placed it upon his lap. The Prophet ﷺ began to wipe the dust from Sa'd's face and clothes, saying, "Sa'd, how sweet your aroma is! How beautiful your face is and you are certainly most beloved to Allah and His Messenger." The Messenger of Allah ﷺ laughed shortly after weeping for Sa'd. He then turned his face from Sa'd saying, "By the Lord of the Ka'bah, the *Ḥawḍ* has arrived. Its length is the distance between Sana'a to Busra. Its border is adorned with pearls and sapphires as the number of stars in the night sky. Its water is extremely white milk made from honey. Whoever drinks from it will never thirst again." The Companions asked: "Messenger of Allah, we saw you weeping and then you were laughing. We also noticed that you turned your back upon Sa'd." The Prophet ﷺ responded, "As for my tears they were out of yearning for Sa'd. While my laughter was because I was pleased for him with his rank with Allah and the honour Allah bestowed upon him. As for my act of turning my back it was because I saw his wives from *al-Ḥur al-'Īn* rushing towards Sa'd. Their shins were unveiled and their anklets were visible, so I turned my sight away from them out of shyness." The Prophet ﷺ ordered that Sa'd's armour and belongings be gathered and said to his Companions, "Take these to Sa'd's wife and tell her that Allah the Sublime and Majestic has married him to a woman better than your women. Sa'd's belongings are his inheritance."[42]

Julaybīb

Ibn al-Jawzī reported that Julaybīb was a black man from the *Anṣār*. Ibn Ḥibbān narrates on the authority of Abū Barzah al-Aslamī: Julaybīb was from the *Anṣār*. He used to go and visit women and talk with them. Abū Barzah said to his wife, "Do not let Julaybīb come and visit you." If the Companions of the Prophet ﷺ had an unmarried woman they would not marry her off until they knew if the Prophet ﷺ was in need of her. One day, the Messenger of Allah ﷺ said to a man from the *Anṣār*, "So-and-so, marry me your daughter." He said, "Certainly and what an excellent husband you are!" He replied. "It is not for myself that I intend her," said the Prophet ﷺ. "Then who?" The man asked. "It is for Julaybīb," responded the Prophet ﷺ. The man said, "Messenger of Allah, I would need to consult my daughter's mother."

---

[42] Ibn al-Jawzī, 1998, pp. 136-141.

The man went to her and said, "The Messenger of Allah ﷺ asked for our daughter's hand in marriage." "Certainly and what an excellent husband he is!" said the mother excitedly. "It is not for himself that he intends her," said the father. "Then who?" the mother asked. "It is Julaybīb." "My daughter marrying Julaybīb! Definitely not! I swear by Allah I will not marry my daughter to Julaybīb!" said the mother. As the father of the girl was about to leave for the Prophet ﷺ, the girl from her chamber said to her mother, "Who is it that requested my hand?" "The Messenger of Allah ﷺ," they replied. "Do you dare reject the proposal of the Messenger of Allah ﷺ! Give me to the Messenger of Allah ﷺ! Surely he will never let me perish." The father then went to the Prophet ﷺ and said, "My daughter's affair is as you please," so he married her to Julaybīb.

Isḥāq ibn 'Abdullāh ibn Abī Ṭalḥah said [to Thābit, the narrator of this report], "Do you know what he supplicated for her?" He said, "What did he supplicate for her?" "He said, 'O Allah shower abundant goodness upon them both and do not make their lives full of toil and hardship.'"

Thābit then went on to say: "The Prophet ﷺ married her to him. After a military expedition, the Prophet ﷺ asked his Companions, 'Have you lost anyone?' They said, 'No.' The Prophet ﷺ said to them, 'But I have lost Julaybīb. So look for him among the dead.' They searched until they found his body beside seven whom he had killed and who had killed him. The Messenger of Allah ﷺ said, 'Did he kill seven people and then they killed him? This one is from me and I am from him,' saying it seven times. The Messenger of Allah ﷺ placed him upon his forearms and he had no other bier but the forearms of the Messenger of Allah ﷺ until he placed him in his grave." Thābit said: "There was not an unmarried woman amongst the *Anṣār* more in demand in marriage than her."[43]

---

[43] Ibn Ḥibbān, *dhikru mā yustaḥabbu lil-mar'i 'inda't-tazwīj an yaṭluba'd-dīn dūna'l-māl fi'l-'aqd 'alā waladihi aw 'alā nafsih,* No. 4035; Ibn al-Jawzī, 1998, p. 143.

Aslam al-Aswad

Ibn Isḥāq reports:

> (Aslam) al-Aswad came to the Prophet ﷺ with his flock of sheep as he was besieging Khaybar. He was the hired servant of a Jew there. He asked the Prophet ﷺ to explain Islam to him, and when he did so he accepted it, for the Prophet ﷺ never thought too little of anyone to invite him to accept Islam. Having become a Muslim he told the Prophet ﷺ that he was the hired servant of the owner of the sheep which were entrusted to his care, and what was he to do with them? He told him to strike the sheep in the face and they would go back to their owner. So Al-Aswad got up and took a handful of pebbles and threw them in their faces, saying, "Go back to your master, for I will look after you no more." They went off in a body as though someone were driving them, until they went into the fort. Afterwards he advanced to the fort with the Muslims and was struck by a stone and was killed, never having prayed a single prayer. He was brought to the Prophet ﷺ, who was accompanied by a number of his Companions, turned towards him and then turned away. When they asked why, he said, "He has with him now his two wives from the dark-eyed *ḥūrīs.*" Ibn Isḥāq said that he was informed by 'Abdullāh ibn Abū Najīḥ that, when a martyr is slain, his two wives from the dark-eyed *ḥūrīs* pet him, wiping the dust from his face, saying "May Allah put dust on the face of the man who put dust on your face, and slay him who slew you."[44]

Abū Bakrah

Abū Bakrah, literally 'the Father of the Pulley', was an Abyssinian Companion. His name was Nāfi'. Abū Bakrah was the servant of Al-

---

[44] Ibn Isḥāq, 2007, p. 519; As-Suyūṭī, 2004, p. 88.

Ḥārith ibn Kaldah ath-Thaqafī, and his mother was Sumayyah, the servant girl of Al-Ḥārith. He embraced Islam but was unable to meet the Messenger of Allah ﷺ. When the Muslim army surrounded Ṭā'if, a man called out, "Any slave who comes out to us from the fortress is a free man." A group of slaves emerged and Abū Bakrah was among them. The place of his descent was called Bakrah, hence the agnomen Abū Bakrah. Abū Bakrah used to say: "I am your brother in religion. I am the *mawlā* (freed slave) of the Messenger of Allah ﷺ. If people refuse to accept my lineage, know that I am Nāfi' ibn Masrūḥ, the Abyssinian!" Abū Bakrah's sons were honoured in Baṣrah for the great extent of their knowledge, wealth and inheritance. Al-Ḥasan used to say, "There was no one in Baṣrah from amongst the Companions better than 'Imrān ibn Ḥuṣayn and Abū Bakrah." Abū Bakrah withdrew himself from the *fitnah* on the Day of the Camel. Al-Bukhārī narrates on the authority of Abū Bakrah: "Allah benefitted me on the Day of the Camel by something I heard from the Messenger of Allah ﷺ, after I almost joined with the people of the Camel to fight along with them. When it reached the Messenger of Allah ﷺ that the people of Persia had put the daughter of Kisrā as their monarch over them, he said, 'No people will be successful who entrust their affairs to a woman.'"[45]

Sālim, Abū Ḥudhayfah's *mawlā* (freed slave)

Before Islam, Sālim was known as Sālim ibn Abī Ḥudhayfah, until the Qur'ānic verse prohibiting adoption was revealed.[46] Sālim was then called Sālim the *mawlā* of Abū Ḥudhayfah. Sālim was one of the most knowledgeable reciters of the Qur'ān and he used to lead the Companions in prayer.

---

45 Al-Bukhārī, *kitāb al-maghāzī, bāb kitāb an-Nabiyyi ṣalla'llāhu 'alayhi wa sallama ilā Kisrā wa Qayṣar,* No. 3614, *kitāb al-fitan, bāb al-fitnah allatī tamūju kamawj al-baḥr,* No. 6686. *See also* Ibn Ḥibbān, Al-Ḥākim, At-Tirmidhī, An-Nisā'ī, Aḥmad, Al-Bayhaqī, As-Suyūṭī, 2004, pp. 87-88 and Ibn al-Jawzī, 1998, p. 133.

46 Sūrat al-Aḥzāb 33:5.

'Umar ibn al-Khaṭṭāb ﷺ said, "If Sālim the freed slave of Hudhyfah is made an Imam in prayer and my Lord the sublime and majestic asked me 'Why did you do that?' I would respond 'O my Lord, I heard your Prophet ﷺ say 'Allah loves the truth of the hearts.''"[47] Al-Ḥākim narrated on the authority of 'Ā'ishah ﷺ: "I was late coming to the Messenger of Allah ﷺ one night." He asked me "Where were you?" I replied, "We were listening to the recitation of a man from your Companions in the mosque. I have not heard a voice like his nor a recitation from any of your Companions." So he stood up and I stood up as well, until he listened to the man's recitation. Then he turned towards me and said, "This is Sālim, the *mawlā* of Abū Ḥudhayfah. All praise is due to Allah Who placed a man like him in my community."[48] Abū Nu'aym narrated: "At the Battle of Yamāmah, Sālim took the standard of the Muslims in his right hand. Later on, his hand was cut off, so he took the standard in his left, which was also cut off. Then he clasped the standard upon his chest and began to recite:[49] "*Muhammad is only a Messenger and he has been preceded by other Messengers. If he were to die or be killed, would you turn on your heels? Those who turn on their heels do not harm Allah in any way. Allah will recompense the thankful.*"[50] Al-Ḥākim narrated on the authority of 'Alqamah ibn 'Abdullāh who said: The Messenger of Allah ﷺ said, "Take the Qur'ān from four people: from 'Abdullāh ibn Mas'ūd, Mu'ādh, Ubayy and Sālim, the freed slave of Abū Ḥudhayfah."[51] Zayd ibn Thābit said: When Sālim was martyred, it was said, "A quarter of the Qur'ān has gone."[52] 'Umar ibn al-Khaṭṭāb ﷺ said to his companions, "Make a wish." One said, "I wish this house

---

47 Ibn al-Jawzī, 1998, p. 120.

48 Al-Ḥākim, *dhikr manāqib Sālim mawlā Abī Ḥudhayfah, raḍiya'llāhu ta'ālā 'anhu,* No. 5001.

49 Ibn al-Jawzī, 1998, pp. 120-121.

50 Sūrah Āli 'Imrān 3:144.

51 Al-Ḥākim, *dhikr manāqib Sālim mawlā Abī Ḥudhayfah, raḍiya'llāhu ta'ālā 'anhu,* No. 4999.

52 Al-Ḥākim, *dhikr manāqib Sālim mawlā Abī Ḥudhayfah, raḍiya'llāhu ta'ālā 'anhu,* No. 5004.

was full of gold so that I could spend it in the way of Allah and give *ṣadaqah.* A man said, "I wish it was full of chrysolite and jewels so I could spend it in the way of Allah and give *ṣadaqah.*" Then 'Umar ※ said, "Make a wish." They said, "We do not know, *Amīr al-Mu'minīn!*" 'Umar ※ said, "I wish it was full of men like Abū 'Ubaydah ibn al-Jarrāḥ, Mu'ādh ibn Jabal, Sālim, the *mawlā* of Abū Ḥudhayfah and Ḥudhayfah ibn al-Yamān."[53] Sālim was martyred in the Battle of Yamāmah in the twelfth year of the *hijrah* (632CE), and his head was found at the foot of Abū Ḥudhayfah or the foot of Abū Ḥudhayfah was found by his head.[54]

Shuqrān, the *mawlā* of the Prophet ※

Shuqrān's real name was Ṣāliḥ ibn 'Adawī, and Shuqrān was his nickname. Shuqrān was an Abyssinian slave, owned by 'Abd ar-Raḥmān ibn 'Awf. Then 'Abd ar-Raḥmān gave Shuqrān to the Messenger of Allah ※ as a gift. It is also said that the Prophet ※ bought Shuqrān and then freed him. The Prophet ※ used to urge people to take care of Shuqrān. Shuqrān witnessed the ritual washing of the body of the Prophet ※ after he died. Shuqrān said, "By Allah, I placed the fabric with a pile (*qaṭīfah*) beneath the Messenger of Allah ※ in the grave."[55]

Muhja'

The Prophet ※ said, "The leaders of the blacks are four: Luqmān the Abyssinian, the Negus, Bilāl and Muhja'."[56] Muhja' was one of the *Muhājirūn* (Emigrants). He was the first Muslim to be martyred in the

---

[53]   Al-Ḥākim, *dhikr manāqib Sālim mawlā Abī Ḥudhayfah, raḍiya'llāhu ta'ālā 'anhu,* No. 5005.

[54]   Al-Ḥākim, *dhikr manāqib Sālim mawlā Abī Ḥudhayfah, raḍiya'llāhu ta'ālā 'anhu,* No. 5000.

[55]   At-Tirmidhī, *abwāb al-janā'iz 'an Rasūlillāh ṣalla'llāhu 'alayhi wa sallama, bāb mā jā'a fī ath-thawb al-wāḥid yulqā taḥta al-mayyiti fī al-qabr,* No. 1052; As-Suyūṭī, 2004, p. 86.

[56]   As-Suyūṭī, 2004, p. 52; Ibn 'Asākir, vol. 10, No. 462. Al-Ḥākim narrates it without mention of the Negus, *dhikr Bilāl ibn Rabāh mu'adhdhin Rasūlillāh ṣalla'llāhu 'alayhi wa sallama,* No. 5242. He declared it *ṣaḥīḥ.*

Battle of Badr. He was killed by a stray arrow whilst he was in the army ranks. Muhja' was an extremely pious man who worshipped Allah constantly. It is said that the verse: *"Do not chase away those who call on their Lord morning and evening, seeking His Face"*[57] was revealed about Muhja'.[58] In his *tafsīr* on the *ayah*, *"Alif Lam Mim. Do people imagine that they will be left to say, 'We have iman' and will not be tested? We tested those before them so that Allah would know the truthful and would know the liars"*[59], Al-Qurṭubī said: Muqātil said, "It was revealed about Muhja', the freed slave of 'Umar ibn al-Khaṭṭāb who was the first of the Muslims to be killed on the day of Badr; 'Āmir ibn al-Ḥaḍramī hit him with an arrow and killed him. The Prophet ﷺ said on that day, "The chief of the martyrs is Muhja', and he is the first of this Ummah who will be called to the door of the Garden."[60]

Mugīth

Al-Bukhārī narrated on the authority of Ibn 'Abbās, "The husband of Barīrah was a black slave called Mugīth. It is as if I can see Mugīth now following Barīrah in the side streets of Madīnah, weeping, his tears flowing over his beard." The Prophet ﷺ said to 'Abbās, "'Abbās! Are you not amazed by the love of Mugīth for Barīrah and Barīrah's hatred for Mugīth?" The Prophet ﷺ said to Barīrah, "If only you would take him back." She said, "Messenger of Allah ﷺ, are you ordering me?" He said, "I am only interceding." She responded, "I have no need of him."[61]

Ju'āl

Al-Ḥākim relates on the authority of Anas: A black man came to the Prophet ﷺ and said "Messenger of Allah ﷺ! I am a black man with

---

57 Sūrat al-An'ām 6:52.

58 Ibn al-Jawzī, 1998, p. 130; As-Suyūṭī, 2004, p. 85-86.

59 Sūrat al-'Ankabūt 29:1-2.

60 Al-Qurṭubī, 2009, p. 216.

61 Ibn al-Jawzī, 1998, pp. 134–135; Al-Bukhārī, *kitāb aṭ-ṭalāq, bāb shafā'at an-Nabiyyi ṣalla'llāhu 'alayhi wa sallama, 'alā zawj Barīrah*, No. 4979.

a rotten smell, an ugly face and I have no property. If I fight those people until I am killed, where will I be?" he replied "In the Garden." So he fought until he was killed. The Prophet ﷺ came to him and said, "Allah has illuminated your face, sweetened your smell and increased your wealth." He then said to this one or someone else, "Indeed I have just seen his wife from *al-Ḥur al-'Īn* removing the wool garment from his body and getting in between him and his garment."[62]

Banū Arifdah

Al-Bukhārī narrates on the authority of 'Ā'ishah ﵂: The Messenger of Allah ﷺ came to see me whilst two girls were with me singing the songs of *Bu'ath.*[63] The Prophet ﷺ lay down on the bed and turned his face away. Then (my father) Abū Bakr came and spoke to me harshly saying, "The musical instruments of Shaytan near the Prophet ﷺ!" The Messenger of Allah ﷺ turned his face towards him and said, "Leave them." When he became inattentive, I signalled to the girls to go out and they left. It was a day of *'Īd* (celebration) and the blacks were playing with shields and spears; so either I asked the Prophet ﷺ or he asked me, "Would you like to see?" I said, "Yes." Then he made me stand behind him, my cheek on his cheek while he was saying, "Carry on, Banī Arfidah." Until when I became bored, he said, "Is that enough for you?" I said, "Yes." He said, "Go on."[64]

Yassār al-Aswad

Yassār al-Aswad was a black Abyssinian man who used to clean the mosque of the Prophet ﷺ in Madīnah. Ibn al-Jawzī reported on the authority of Abū Hurayrah: I went in to visit the Prophet ﷺ and he said

---

[62] Al-Ḥākim, *kitāb al-jihād,* No. 2463. Al-Bayhaqī also cites it as does Ibn an-Nūḥās, 2002, pp. 726-727. The wording here is that of Al-Ḥākim.

[63] A story about the war between the two tribes of the *Anṣār*, the Khazraj and the Aws, before Islam.

[64] Al-Bukhārī, *kitāb al-'īdayn, bāb al-ḥirāb wa'd-daraqi yawma'l-'īd,* No. 907; Muslim, *al-'īdayn, bāb ar-rukhṣah fi'l-la'b alladhī lā Messenger of Allah'ṣiyata fīhi*, No. 829.

to me, "Abū Hurayrah, a man from the people whom Allah will use to defend the people of the earth will come in to see me right now through this door." Soon after that an Abyssinian man appeared through the door. The Messenger of Allah ﷺ said, "That is him, Welcome, Yassār! Welcome, Yassār! Welcome, Yassār!"[65]

Ayman al-Ḥabashī

Ayman al-Ḥabashī was the son of Umm Ayman and the half-brother of the esteemed Companion, Usāmah ibn Zayd. Ayman was among the Companions who held firm and heroically defended the Prophet ﷺ at the Battle of Ḥunayn. He died as a martyr whilst defending the Prophet ﷺ.[66]

Anjashah

Al-Bukhārī reports: The Prophet ﷺ had a camel driver called Anjashah, who drove them by singing to them and he had a good voice, so the Prophet ﷺ said to him, "Be gentle, Anjashah, don't break the crystal glasses." Qatādah said, "Meaning, the weak women."[67]

Khālid ibn al-Ḥawārī al-Ḥabashī

Khālid ibn al-Hawarī was a pious Abyssinian Companion. When death was approaching Khālid, he said, "Wash me twice: one for the ritual purification wash (*janābah*) and the other for my death."[68]

Dhū Mukhbar

Dhū Mukhbar came to Madīnah with a group of Abyssinians who had embraced Islam. Dhū Mukhbar accompanied the Prophet ﷺ and attended him.[69]

---

65 Ibn al-Jawzī, 1998, p. 142.

66 Ibn Isḥāq, 2007, pp. 586-587; As-Suyūṭī, 2004, p. 101.

67 Al-Bukhārī, *kitāb al-adab, bāb al-ma'ārīḍ mandūḥah 'an al-kadhib,* No. 5857.

68 As-Suyūṭī, 2004, p. 89.

69 As-Suyūṭī, 2004, p. 90.

Dhū Muhdam

Dhū Muhdam was an Abyssinian Companion who went to Madīnah to accompany the Prophet ﷺ along with Dhū Mukhbar.[70]

'Āṣim al-Ḥabashī

'Āṣim was the servant boy of Zar'ah. One day, Zar'ah took him to the Prophet ﷺ and said, "Messenger of Allah ﷺ! I have bought this man and I would love if you could name him and make supplication for him to receive divine blessings (*barakah*)." The Prophet ﷺ asked the man, "What is your name?" The man replied, "Aṣram."[71] The Prophet ﷺ said, "But you are a farmer. What name do you prefer?" "I would like to be known as a shepherd," the man answered. "Therefore your name is 'Āṣim."[72] The Prophet ﷺ then took 'Āṣim by the hand.[73]

Nābil al-Ḥabashī

Nābil was the father of Ayman ibn Nābil. Nābil was a loyal Companion of the Prophet ﷺ and narrated some prophetic traditions.[74]

Abū Laqīṭ al-Ḥabashī

Abū Laqīṭ was a freed slave of the Prophet ﷺ. He died during the caliphate of 'Umar ﷺ.[75]

Rabāḥ

Rabāḥ was one of the servants of the Prophet ﷺ. When the Prophet ﷺ separated temporarily from his wives, Rabāḥ stayed with him and attended him.[76]

---

70 As-Suyūṭī, 2004, p. 90.
71 Aṣram means 'most harsh and severe'.
72 'Āṣim means 'protector and guardian'.
73 As-Suyūṭī, 2004, pp. 90-91.
74 As-Suyūṭī, 2004, p. 91.
75 As-Suyūṭī, 2004, p. 91.
76 See Muslim, *kitāb aṭ-ṭalāq, bāb fi'l-īlā' wa'tizāl an-nisā' wa takhyīrihinna wa qawlihi ta'ālā "wa in taẓāharā 'alayhi..."*, No. 1479.

Female Companions

Māriyah the Copt 🕮

Māriyah al-Qibṭiyyah 🕮 was the mother of the last born child of the Prophet 🕮, Ibrāhīm, who died in infancy. Māriyah's mother was Greek and her father was a Coptic Egyptian. Māriyah was sent as a gift from Muqawqis, a Byzantine official, to the Prophet 🕮 in Madīnah.[1]

Gift from Muqawqis

The Prophet 🕮 sent a letter to Muqawqis, a Byzantine official, summoning him to Islam. Muqawqis answered evasively, but with his answer the ruler of Egypt sent a rich present of a thousand measures of gold, twenty robes of fine cloth, a mule, a she-ass and, as the crown of the gift, two Coptic Christian slave-girls escorted by an elderly eunuch. The slave girls were sisters, Māriyah and Sīrīn, and both were beautiful, but Māriyah 🕮 was exceptionally so, and the Prophet 🕮 marvelled at her beauty. He gave Sīrīn to Ḥassān ibn Thābit, and lodged Māriyah 🕮 in the nearby house where Ṣafiyyah 🕮 had lived before her apartment adjoining the Mosque was built. There he would visit her both by day and night; but his wives became so openly jealous that she was unhappy, and he then lodged her in Upper

---

[1] Ibn Ḥajar, 1995 and Aṭ-Ṭabarī, 2008, *Tārīkh aṭ-Ṭabarī*.

Mādinah. 'Ā'ishah 🌸, the beloved wife of the Messenger of Allah ﷺ said the following about Māriyah 🌸. "I have never been jealous of a woman as much as I was jealous of Māriyah. That was because she was a beauty among women, curly haired, and the Messenger of Allah ﷺ was delighted with her."[2]

Birth of Ibrāhīm

Māriyah 🌸 gave birth to Ibrāhīm in the month of Dhū al-Ḥijjah in the eighth year after the Hijrah. Māriyah 🌸 was the only woman other than his first wife, Khadījah 🌸, to bear him a child. When Ibrāhīm was born, the angel Jibrīl came to the Prophet ﷺ and addressed him, "Peace be upon you, Abū Ibrāhīm (Father of Ibrāhīm)."[3] Some contemporary scholars are of the opinion that he ﷺ married Māriyah 🌸, however the majority of classical scholars say that he did not.[4]

Death of Ibrāhīm

Ibrāhīm died in Rabī' al-Awwal in the tenth year of the Hijrah when he was only sixteen months old. When Ibrāhīm was dying, the eyes of the Messenger of Allah ﷺ flowed with tears. 'Abd ar-Raḥmān ibn 'Awf said to him, "Even you, Messenger of Allah!" He said, "Ibn 'Awf, they are a mercy." He added, "The eye flows with tears, the heart grieves but we do not say anything except that which pleases our Lord. And we are indeed saddened by separation from you, Ibrāhīm."[5] Al-Bukhārī narrates: The sun was eclipsed in the lifetime of the Messenger of Allah ﷺ on the day of Ibrāhīm's death. So the people

---

[2]   'Abd al-Ghaffār, 2003, p. 414, citing Ibn Sa'd, *tasmiyah an-nisā' al-muslimāt wa'l-muhājirāt min Quraysh wa'l-Anṣāriyyāt al-mubāyi'āt wa gharā'ib nisā' al-'arab wa ghayrihim, dhikr Māriyah Umm Ibrāhīm ibn Rasūli'llāhi ṣalla'llāhu 'alayhi wa sallam.*
[3]   Al-Bazzār and Al-Haythamī.
[4]   Ibn Ḥajar, 1995 and Aṭ-Ṭabarī, 2008, *Tārīkh aṭ-Ṭabarī.*
[5]   Al-Bukhārī, *kitāb al-janā'iz, bāb qawl an-Nabiyyi ṣalla'llāhu 'alayhi wa sallama "innā bika lamuḥzanūn"*, No. 1241.

said that the sun was eclipsed because of the death of Ibrāhīm. The Messenger of Allah ﷺ said, "The sun and the moon are not eclipsed because of the death of anyone or his life, so when you see it, pray and supplicate Allah."[6]

Death of Māriyah ﵂

Abū Bakr and 'Umar ﵄ used to support Māriyah ﵂ financially after the death of the Prophet ﷺ and she died five years after him. 'Umar gathered the people for her funeral and prayed the funeral prayer over her in the cemetery of al-Baqī'.[7]

Umm Ayman

Umm Ayman was the *kunyah* of a black slave from Abyssinia whose name was Barakah. Umm Ayman originally belonged to the father of the Prophet ﷺ who inherited her after his father's passing. Umm Ayman used to look after the Messenger of Allah ﷺ when he was an infant after the passing of Amīnah, the mother of the Prophet ﷺ. The Messenger of Allah ﷺ freed Umm Ayman when he married his first wife, Khadījah ﵂. After her emancipation, Umm Ayman married 'Abdullāh ibn Zayd and gave birth to Ayman from whom she derived her *kunyah*. One day, after the death of her first husband, the Prophet ﷺ said to his Companions, "Whoever wishes to marry a woman from the people of the Garden, let him marry Umm Ayman."[8] Upon hearing this, Zayd ibn al-Ḥārithah proposed to her and married her. In due time, she gave birth to Usāmah ibn Zayd. The Prophet ﷺ used to say, "Umm Ayman is my mother after my mother."[9] The Prophet ﷺ used to honour Umm Ayman and jest with her from time

---

6 Al-Bukhārī, *kitāb al-kusūf, bāb aṣ-ṣalāh fī kusūf ash-shams,* No. 996.
7 Ibn Ḥajar, 1995 and Aṭ-Ṭabarī, 2008, *Tārīkh aṭ-Ṭabarī.*
8 Ibn Sa'd 8:224.
9 Ibn Ḥajar, 1995.

to time. One day she asked, "I need a riding beast." The Prophet ﷺ replied, "I will give you the baby of a camel to ride on." "No, that's no good, a baby camel would not be able to carry me," Umm Ayman said. "I will not give you any riding beast except a baby camel, after all isn't every camel the baby of another camel," he ﷺ said.[10] Anas said: "Abū Bakr said to 'Umar, after the passing of the Messenger of Allah ﷺ, 'Let's go and visit Umm Ayman, just as the Messenger of Allah ﷺ used to visit her.'" [Anas said] "When we went to her she cried. They asked her, 'What makes you weep? Do you not know that what is with Allah is better for His Messenger ﷺ?' She replied, 'I do not weep because I do not know that what is with Allah is better for His Messenger ﷺ, but I cry because the descent of revelation from heaven has stopped.' Both Abū Bakr and 'Umar broke into tears upon hearing this."[11] Umm Ayman was present at the Battle of Uḥud. She treated the injured *mujāhids* (combatants) and gave them water. She also witnessed the Battles of Khaybar and Ḥunayn. She died during the caliphate of 'Uthmān ؓ.[12]

Umm Zufar

Umm Zufar's name was said to be Sa'īrah al-Asadiyyah but some said it was Shaqīrah. Al-Bukhārī and Muslim narrated that 'Aṭā ibn Abī Rabāḥ said: Ibn 'Abbās said to me: "Should I not show you a woman from the inhabitants of the Garden?" "Certainly!" I replied. "That black woman over there; she went to the Prophet ﷺ and said, 'I suffer from epileptic fits and uncover myself. Please pray to Allah for me.' He said, 'If you

---

10 Ibn al-Jawzī, 1998, p. 149.

11 Muslim, *kitāb faḍā'il aṣ-ṣaḥābah raḍiya'llāhu 'anhum, bāb min faḍā'il Umm Ayman raḍiya'llāhu 'anhā*, No. 2453.

12 Ibn Ḥajar; Ibn al-Jawzī, 1998, pp. 148-149; As-Suyūṭī, 2004, pp. 93-96.

13 Al-Bukhārī, *kitāb al-marḍā, bāb faḍl man yuṣra'u min ar-rīḥ*, No. 5328; and Muslim, *al-birr wa'ṣ-ṣilah wa'l-ādāb, bāb thawāb al-mu'min fīmā yuṣībuhu min maraḍin aw ḥuzn...*, No. 2576.

want you can be patient and you will have the Garden or if you want I can pray to Allah to cure you.' She said, 'I will be patient.' Then she said, 'I become uncovered; please pray for me that I do not uncover myself.' And so he supplicated for her."[13]

Barīrah

Barīrah was a black slave woman from the *Anṣār*. She was married to a black slave called Mugīth. She asked 'Ā'ishah ﵂ to help her in purchasing her freedom. 'Ā'ishah ﵂ reported that the Messenger of Allah ﷺ said to her about Barīrah, "Buy her and set her free."[14] So 'Ā'ishah ﵂ bought Barīrah from her owners and freed her. The Messenger of Allah ﷺ gave Barīrah the choice of remaining married to Mugīth, who was a slave, or separating from him and she chose to separate from him. 'Ā'ishah ﵂ reported that when the Messenger of Allah ﷺ gave Barīrah the choice[15] he told her, "If your husband approaches you then you can choose whether you want to get back with him or not." Barīrah's departure broke Mugīth's heart. The Prophet ﷺ said to Barīrah, "If only you would take him back." She said, "Messenger of Allah ﷺ, are you ordering me?" He said, "I am only interceding." She responded, "I have no need of him."[16]

Umm Miḥjan

Umm Miḥjan is said to have been the name of an elderly black woman who used to clean the mosque of the Prophet ﷺ in Madīnah. Abū Hurayrah narrated that a black man or a black woman used to look after the mosque and then died. The Prophet ﷺ asked about him and

---

14 Al-Bukhārī, *kitāb ash-shurūṭ, bāb al-mukātabah wa mā lā yaḥillu min ash-shurūṭ allatī tukhālifu kitāba'llāh*, No. 2584.

15 It was by this act that it was established that when a slave woman who is married to a slave is set free, she then has the choice of whether to remain in the marriage - Ed.

16 Al-Bukhārī, *kitāb aṭ-ṭalāq, bāb shafā'at an-Nabiyyi ṣalla'llāhu 'alayhi wa sallama, 'alā zawj Barīrah,* No. 4979.

they said, "He died." He said, "Why did you not inform me of it? Show me his grave" or he said, "her grave" and he went to her grave and prayed over her.[17]

A singing slave-girl

The Messenger of Allah ﷺ went on one of his military expeditions; then when he returned, a black slave-girl came to him and said, "Messenger of Allah, I had vowed that if Allah returned you in full health, I would beat the tambourine before you and sing." So the Messenger of Allah ﷺ said to her, "If you have vowed then beat, otherwise no." So she began to beat and then Abū Bakr ؓ came in while she was beating, then ʿAlī ؓ came in while she was beating, then ʿUthmān ؓ came in while she was beating. Then ʿUmar ؓ came, and she put the tambourine under her seat and sat on it. The Messenger of Allah ﷺ said, "Indeed Shaytan is afraid of you, ʿUmar!"[18]

---

[17]   Al-Bukhārī, kitāb aṣ-ṣalāh, bāb kans al-masjid wa'ltiqāṭ al-khariq wa'l-qadhā wa'l-ʿīdān, No. 446. See also hadith Nos. 448 and 1272; Muslim, al-janā'iz, bāb aṣ-ṣalāh ʿala'l-qabr, No. 956. There was some doubt as to whether the person who looked after the mosque was a man or a woman, but the stronger position seems to be that it was a woman called Umm Miḥjan - Ed.

[18]   At-Tirmidhī, kitāb al-manāqib ʿan Rasūlillāh ṣalla'llāhu ʿalayhi wa sallama, No. 3842.

13

Religious Scholars and Explorers

'Aṭā ibn Abī Rabāḥ

'Aṭā ibn Abī Rabāḥ (d. 733) was of Abyssinian origin and was born in Makkah during the caliphate of 'Uthmān ibn 'Affān ﷺ. 'Aṭā's father's name was Abū Rabāḥ Aslam. 'Aṭā was the slave of a woman from the tribe of Khaytham and, in addition to fulfilling his domestic duties, he used to study. After seeing 'Aṭā's ardent love for religious knowledge, 'Aṭā's mistress freed him so that he could pursue his desire for religious studies. 'Aṭā mastered many of the Islamic sciences and grew in prominence to become one of the greatest scholars of the *Salaf* (the early generations). 'Aṭā was an erudite scholar, trustworthy jurist and hadith specialist. He studied the Islamic sciences under the tutelage of Ibn 'Umar, Abū Sa'īd, Abū Hurayrah, Ibn 'Abbās and many other Companions ﷺ, but mostly under Ibn 'Abbās. 'Aṭā said that he met two hundred Companions of the Messenger of Allah ﷺ. He was known for his *taqwā* as well as his scholarship and was highly revered. He was described as being dark-skinned, lame and paralysed with impaired vision. Towards the end of his life, 'Aṭā lost his sight entirely. Imam ash-Shāfi'ī, the celebrated jurist and eponym of the Shafi'ite school of jurisprudence said, "The sessions for issuing religious edicts (*fatwā*) in the Sacred Mosque of Makkah were under the supervision of Ibn 'Abbās. After Ibn 'Abbās, this responsibility and honour was given to

'Aṭā ibn Abī Rabāḥ." As-Suyūṭī narrates on the authority of 'Umar ibn Sa'd ibn Abū Ḥusayn that his mother was sent to Ibn 'Abbās to ask him a question about the *dīn*. Ibn 'Abbās informed the people, "People of Makkah, are you gathering around me (seeking edicts) when you have 'Aṭā in your midst?" 'Aṭā performed the pilgrimage seventy times and lived for a hundred years.[1]

Sa'īd ibn Jubayr

Sa'īd ibn Jubayr (d. 714) was a scholar from the early generations of Muslims (*Salaf*). Originally from Abyssinia, Sa'īd studied the Islamic sciences under several Companions, most notably Ibn 'Abbās. A leading jurist of his time, Sa'īd was not only a scholar but also an Islamic combatant (*mujāhid*). At the Battle of Jamājim in 699, Sa'īd ibn Jubayr joined Ibn Ash'ath and his followers, including 100,000 from amongst the *mawālī*, or freed slaves, to take on the army of the tyrannical Iraqi governor, Al-Ḥajjāj ibn Yūsuf. The revolt of Ibn Ash'ath was brutally put down and Sa'īd was forced to flee to the outskirts of Makkah. Despite living in exile, Sa'īd continued to return secretly to Makkah and Kufa to perform the pilgrimage and issue *fatwās*. Sa'īd was finally apprehended and brought before Al-Ḥajjāj. Before his execution, Sa'īd supplicated Allah to bring an end to Al-Ḥajjāj's tyranny. Al-Ḥajjāj lost his sanity and died within a month of Sa'īd's execution.[2]

Ibn Abī Zayd al-Qayrawānī

Abū Muḥammad 'Abdullāh ibn Abī Zayd al-Qayrawānī (d. 996) was a prominent Berber traditionalist, educationalist and jurist from al-Qayrawān in Tunisia. Nicknamed 'the younger Mālik' after the eponym of the Mālikī school of jurisprudence, Ibn Abī Zayd was a

---

[1] As-Suyūṭī, 2004, pp. 101-104; Ibn al-Jawzī, 1998, pp. 153-158.
[2] Al-Hāshimī, 1993, pp. 7-22.

strong advocate of Mālikī *fiqh*. He possessed a prodigious memory and had an extensive knowledge of the Islamic sciences, to which his books are ample testimony. In addition to his writings, Ibn Abī Zayd had great *taqwā*, and was scrupulous and intelligent. His companions were noble and many people took knowledge from him. Ibn Abī Zayd was also a prolific writer; he wrote over thirty-five books and treatises about Islamic theology, jurisprudence and etiquettes, and composed an abridgement of the *Mudawwanah,* which is a summation of the Mālikī school and Imam Mālik's *fatwās*. His most famous work is *Ar-Risālah* ['The Epistle'], a treatise on Islamic *tawḥīd* and *fiqh*, and was written when he was only seventeen years old.[3]

Shihāb ad-Dīn al-Qarāfī

Shihāb ad-Dīn Abū al-'Abbās Aḥmad ibn Idrīs aṣ-Ṣanhājī al-Bahnasī al-Miṣrī al-Qarāfī (d. 1285) was a Mālikī jurist and legal theoretician of Berber (Ṣanhājah) origin. Al-Qarāfī was born in the Bahnasa district of Upper Egypt around 1228. He is considered by many to be the greatest Mālikī legal theoretician of the thirteenth century; his writings and influence on Islamic legal theory (*uṣūl al-fiqh*) spread throughout the Muslim world. His insistence on the full range of *fiqh* principles shows the importance of some of the lesser known principles in determining the proper course of action. For example, his views on the common good (*maṣlaḥah*) and custom, which are core principles of Mālikī *fiqh*, provide means to accommodate the space-time differential between modern and pre-modern realities. The most important of his many works are: *Adh-Dhakhīrah* ['The Stored Treasure'], an opus on Mālikī jurisprudence, *Al-Furūq* ['The Differences'], *Nafā'is al-uṣūl* ['Gems of Legal Theory'], and *Kitāb al-iḥkām fī tamyīz al-fatawā 'an al-aḥkām wa taṣarrufāt al-qāḍī wa'l-imām* ['The Book of Perfecting the Distinction

[3] See 'Abū Muḥammad 'Abdullāh Ibn Abī Zayd al-Qayrawānī, 1990, *Kitāb al-Jāmi'*. pp. 52-69.

Between Legal Opinions, Judicial Decisions, and the Discretionary Actions of Judges and Caliphs'].[4]

Muḥammad ibn 'Abd al-Karīm al-Maghīlī

Muḥammad ibn 'Abd al-Karīm al-Maghīlī (d. 1505) was a Berber scholar from Tlemcen, a Saharan city situated in modern-day Algeria. A well-known itinerant scholar, Al-Maghīlī used to advise Muslim rulers on issues confronting Muslim societies from Spain to sub-Saharan Africa. He spent several years teaching and counselling rulers in Hausaland[5] and the Sudanic kingdom of Songhay (in present-day Niger), and wrote a highly influential treatise, *Tāj ad-dīn fī mā yajib 'alā al-mulūk* ['The Crown of Religion Concerning the Obligation of Rulers'], which laid out in detail how a Muslim ruler should govern his subjects. This document had a deep impact on the subsequent history of Islam in West Africa, providing all future Muslim revivers with the essential elements of a manifesto for the struggle for the establishment of the *dīn*. Al-Maghīlī's writings and teachings made a significant contribution to the development of the Islamic revival movements of the nineteenth century. Usman dan Fodio and Askia Muḥammad relied heavily on Al-Maghīlī's writings in their attempts to purify West Africa from idolatry and polytheism and were successful in reviving a fully functioning society and polity whose very substantial effects have endured till today.[6]

Aḥmad Bābā

Abū al-'Abbās Aḥmad ibn Aḥmad at-Takrūrī al-Massufī at-Tinbuktī (d. 1627) was an illustrious West African writer, jurist, scholar, and

4 See Sherman A. Jackson, 1996, *Islamic Law and the State: The Constitutional Jurisprudence of Shihāb ad-Dīn al-Qarāfī*. pp. 1-32.
5 Situated in present-day Northern Nigeria.
6 Glazier, 2001, p. 158.

political provocateur in the area then known as the Western Sudan. Aḥmad Bābā was the son of a noted scholar and teacher, Aḥmad ibn al-Ḥājj Aḥmad ibn 'Umar ibn Muḥammad Aqīṭ. Born at Araouane, he moved to Timbuktu at an early age to study with his father and with a scholar known as Muḥammad Baghayu'u. When Timbuktu was conquered by the Sultan of Morocco in 1591, Bābā was accused of refusing to recognise the Sultan's authority and of sedition. In 1594 he was deported to the Moroccan capital of Marrakech. The conditions of his captivity were liberal, and he was allowed to teach and practice law. His *fatwās* (legal opinions) dating from this period are noted for their clarity of thought and clear exposition of Islamic judicial principles. He also compiled a biographical dictionary of famous Mālikī jurists; this work is still an important source of information concerning the lives of Mālikī jurists and Moroccan religious personalities. When the Sultan of Morocco died in 1603, Aḥmad Bābā was allowed to return to his native city. He spent the last years of his life in scholarly pursuits.[7] Many scholars consider Aḥmad Bābā a *mujaddid*[8] of the seventeenth century.

Usman dan Fodio

His full name was 'Uthmān ibn Muḥammad ibn Fūdī, but he is better known as Usman dan Fodio (d. 1816), and he was an acclaimed West African jurist and theologian. Usman dan Fodio was one of the principal revivers of Islam in Hausaland in Northern Nigeria in the late eighteenth and early ninteenth centuries and founder of the Sokoto Caliphate. He was born in the Hausa state of Gobir, the son of a pious Fulani member of the Qādiriyyah *ṭarīqah*. Dan Fodio received

7 Hunwick, 2006, pp. 32-34.

8 A *mujaddid* according to Islamic tradition is a figure, or one of a number of figures, who appear every one hundred years to revive the *dīn* of Islam - Ed.

a thorough education in Islamic *tawḥīd*, Arabic, and Islamic law, and by 1774 he began his career as an itinerant teacher. During these years, dan Fodio travelled throughout Hausaland, gaining adherents and teaching social reform. His followers, who were later to form the vanguard of his fighting forces, came from all parts of the central lands of the Sudan, which at that time comprised Mali, Chad, Nigeria, and Niger in addition to the present-day nation-state of Sudan. Dan Fodio objected to the non-Islamic practices of the Hausa leaders and continually criticised their rule and questioned the legitimacy of the taxes they imposed on his Fulani brethren. His teaching and the ever-increasing number of his followers throughout Hausaland caused growing alarm among the pagan Hausa chiefs, especially the Sultan of Gobir, who sought to undermine dan Fodio's influence. In 1804, Shehu Usman and his followers were forced to flee for safety from Gobir, in a manner reminiscent of the emigration of the Messenger of Allah ﷺ from Makkah, and proclaimed war against the Hausa chiefs. He was named *Amīr al-Mu'minīn* (Leader of the Faithful) in Gudu. This made him a political as well as a religious leader, giving him the authority to declare and pursue *jihād*. Usman dan Fodio's principal role during the years of war that followed was that of a political, military and spiritual leader, mediator, and chief source of inspiration for his followers. The so-called Fulani War, lasted until 1810, and ended with dan Fodio triumphant. Ruling from Gobir, dan Fodio changed the name of the city to Sokoto. The polity he built became the Sokoto Caliphate. Establishing a centralised government, dan Fodio began a period of economic stability and security in the region. When he retired from political duties in 1811, he worked relentlessly to establish an efficient government grounded in Islamic law. After his death in 1817, Muḥammad Bello, dan Fodio's son, succeeded him as *Amīr al-Mu'minīn* and the ruler of the Sokoto Caliphate. The success of Usman dan Fodio's struggle inspired a number of later West Africans including Seku Amadu, the founder of the Massina Empire, 'Umar Tall, the founder of the Toucouleur Empire, Samory Toure, the founder of the Wassoulou Empire and Modibo Adama, the founder of the Adamawa Empire.[9]

Nana Asmā'u

Nana Asmā'u (d. 1864) was the daughter of the Sokoto Caliph, Usman dan Fodio. Born in Northwest Nigeria, Nana Asmā'u was fluent in Arabic, Fulfulde, Hausa and Tamachek, the language of the Tuareg. She memorised the whole of the Qur'ān and was very knowledgeable in the traditional Islamic sciences. An activist for women's development and education, Nana Asmā'u taught Hausa women the many sciences of the *dīn.* She helped transform her society by re-socialising war refugees and contributed significantly to the Islamic revival process in Northern Nigeria. She was a respected public figure of appreciative authority and was active in politics, education, and social reform; she was a prolific author, popular teacher, and renowned scholar and intellectual. Asmā'u did not accomplish her work in isolation; she was actively involved with her family and the wider community of which it was a part. She became a counsellor to her brother when he took over the Caliphate, and is on record writing instructions to governors and debating with scholars. Over sixty works survive written by Nana Asmā'u over forty years including a large body of poetry, written in Arabic, Fulfulde, and Hausa, all using the Ajami Arabic script. Many of these works are historical narratives, but they also include elegies, laments, and admonitions. Her poems of guidance became tools for teaching both women and men about the fundamental principles of Islam and the Caliphate.[10]

---

[9] See Ibraheem Sulaiman, 2009, *The African Caliphate.*

[10] See Jean Boyd and Beverly B. Mack, 1984, *Collected Works of Nana Asma'u, Daughter of Usman dan Fodiyo (1793-1864).*

Ibn Baṭṭūṭah

Abū 'Abdullāh Muḥammad ibn 'Abdullāh ibn Muḥammad ibn Ibrāhīm ibn Yūsuf ibn al-Lawātī aṭ-Ṭanjī, more commonly known as Ibn Baṭṭūṭah (d. 1369), was a renowned Berber explorer. Ibn Baṭṭūṭah is known for the account of his travels and excursions called *Tuḥfah wa 'ajā'ib al-asfār al-naẓār fī gharā'ib al-amṣār* ['A Gift to those who Contemplate the Wonders of Cities and the Marvels of Travelling']. The manuscript is often referred to as *Ar-Riḥlah* ['The Journey']. Ibn Baṭṭūṭah's journeys lasted for a period of nearly thirty years and covered almost the entirety of the known Muslim world, extending from West Africa to the Middle East and far beyond into Asia and China. Ibn Juzayy, son of the more famous *faqīh* and scholar of *tafsīr* and other Islamic sciences of the same name, to whom Ibn Baṭṭūṭah dictated the travels, said the following about him, "He, who had encompassed the earth with attentive mind and travelled through its cities with observant eye, and who had investigated the diversities of nations and probed the ways of life of Arabs and non-Arabs, thereafter laid down the staff of the much-travelled in this Sublime Residence." After the completion of *Ar-Riḥlah* in 1355, little is known about Ibn Baṭṭūṭah's life other than that he was appointed a judge in Morocco where he died in 1369.[11]

---

[11] Ibn Baṭṭūṭah, 2002, pp. 1-2.

14

Rulers and Kings

Abū al-Misk Kāfūr

Abū al-Misk Kāfūr (d. 968) was a prominent personality of Ikhshidid Egypt and Syria. Originally an Abyssinian slave, Abū al-Misk Kāfūr was promoted to become vizier of Egypt, becoming its *de facto* ruler in 946. After the death of Kāfūr's master, Muḥammad ibn Tughj, Kāfūr succeeded the latter to become the *de jure* ruler of the Ikhshidid domains, Egypt and Southern Syria, until his death in 968. Kāfūr maintained economic stability in Egypt during his reign despite serious setbacks. He was a pious man who gained popularity by being the patron of scholars, writers and poets. Kāfūr's greatest achievement was his successful protection of the Ikhshidid establishment from the Hamdanids in Syria, Fatimids in Northern Africa, Qarmatians in the Arabian Peninsula and Nubians in the south of Egypt.[1]

Mansa Kankan Mūsā

In the annals of African history, no one has left more of an imprint on the outside world than Mansa Kankan Mūsā (d. 1337), the ruler of Mali from 1312 until 1337. Also known as Gongo Mūsā, and in abbreviated

---

[1] See Houtsma, M. Th. and van Donzel, E. [Ed.], 1993, *E. J. Brill's First Encyclopaedia of Islam 1913 -1936.* p. 623.

form Mansa Mūsā, he became one of the most powerful leaders of his time and Mali's name became renowned throughout the world. In the fourteenth century, his name and that of Mali were to become synonymous with opulence, learning and justice. A generous and just ruler, Mūsā is known for his role as a benefactor of Islamic scholarship and architecture. Mūsā was the tenth *mansa* (ruler) of the Mali Empire during its height in the fourteenth century. Mūsā is most noted for his famous pilgrimage to Makkah in 1324. The North African scholar, Al-'Umarī, who visited Cairo a few years after Mansa Mūsā's visit to Cairo en route to Makkah, declared that of all the Muslim rulers of West Africa, Mūsā was "the most powerful, the richest, the most fortunate, the most feared by his enemies and the most able to do good to those around him."[2]

Al-Ḥajj Askiya Muḥammad Toure

Al-Ḥajj[3] Askiya[4] Muḥammad Toure (d. 1538) was a king of the Songhay Empire in the late fifteenth century. The successor of the tyrant Sunni 'Alī Ber, Askiya Toure was much more astute and farsighted than his predecessor had been. He orchestrated a programme of expansion and consolidation that extended the empire from Taghaza in the North to the borders of Yatenga in the South, and from Air in the Northeast to Futa Tooro in Guinea. In addition, Askiya established standardised trade measures and regulations, and initiated the policing of trade routes. He also encouraged learning and literacy, ensuring that Mali's universities produced the most distinguished scholars, many of whom published significant books. Under his tutelage, the eminent scholar, Aḥmad Bābā, wrote numerous treatises on Islamic law, Maḥmūd Kāti

2 See Robin Walker, 2005, *When We Ruled.*

3 The honorific title al-Ḥajj (also el-Ḥajj or el-Hadj) is reserved for a Muslim who has performed the pilgrimage (*ḥajj*) to Makkah.

4 Askiya was the title of the rulers of the Songhay Empire.

authored *Tārīkh al-fattāḥ* ['The History of the Conquests'] and 'Abd ar-Raḥmān as-Sa'dī wrote *Tārīkh as-Sūdān* ['The History of Black Africa']. Due to Askiya Toure's efforts Mali experienced a cultural growth it had never witnessed before, and the whole land flourished as a centre of all things valuable in learning and trade. Askiya Toure is buried in Gao, Eastern Mali.[5]

Idris Alooma

Idris Alooma (d. 1596) was a successful Mai[6] of Bornu in the sixteenth century. Alooma reformed and standardised the judiciary by establishing a system of Islamic courts. He was a devout Muslim and he replaced tribal law with Islamic law, taking a stand against immorality and injustice. Alooma was a patron of learning, encouraging scholars from many other African countries to take up residence in Bornu. He improved navigation on the Yobe River and commissioned the building of longer, flat-bottomed boats for his navy. For land transportation, he imported a much larger number of camels, replacing the dependence on mules, oxen and donkeys. Idris Alooma was also a builder, raising new brick mosques that replaced older buildings in the cities. He also founded a hostel in Makkah for Borno pilgrims. Following the fall of Songhay in 1591, the great Mai became the undisputed champion of the Muslims in the region. The empire became the Borno Caliphate. Idris Alooma's military prowess was outstanding. He was an extraordinary ruler who managed to reunite the Bulala with Kanem and form the Kanem-Bornu Empire for half a century. Maḥmūd Kāti, the great Songhay historian, said that Idris Alooma was amongst the greatest Sultans of the Muslim world.[7]

---

5 See John Hunwick, 2003, *Timbuktu & the Songhay Empire.*

6 Mai is the title given to the king or sultan of Bornu.

7 See Robin Walker, 2005, *When We Ruled.*

Queen Amina Sukhera

Amina Sukhera (d. 1610) was a warrior queen of the royal family of Zazzau. Queen Amina ruled for thirty-four years in the sixteenth and seventeenth centuries. Her domain of Zazzau, a city-state of Hausaland, was eventually renamed Zaria and is the capital of the present-day emirate of Kaduna in Northern Nigeria. Amina was the twenty-fourth *habe,* as the rulers of Zazzau were called. She was born during the reign of her grandfather King Zazzau Nohir in 1533. By the time Amina assumed the throne, following the death of her brother in the tenth year of his rule, she had matured into a fierce warrior and had earned the respect of the Zazzau military. Within three months of inheriting the throne, Queen Amina embarked on what was to be the first in an on-going series of military engagements associated with her rule. She stood in command of an immense military force and personally led the cavalry of Zazzau in a series of campaigns, waging battle continually throughout the course of her reign. She spent the greater part of her reign in warfare. Although the military campaigns of Amina were characterised as efforts to ensure safe passage for Zazzau and other Hausa traders throughout the Saharan region, it proved effective in significantly expanding the limits of Zazzau territory. She came to dominate much of the region known as Hausaland in the mid 1600s.[8]

Modibo Adama

Adama Ardo Hassana (d. 1847), more commonly known as Modibo Adama was a Fulani warrior and scholar who led a struggle into the region of Fumbina (in modern-day Cameroon and Nigeria) in the nineteenth century. As a result of Adama's effort, Islam became the dominant *dīn* in the region. Adama studied in Hausaland and earned the title, 'Modibo' (the learned one) for his scholarship. Upon finishing

8 See Robin Walker, 2005, *When We Ruled.*

his studies, Adama returned home to Gurina and learned of Usman dan Fodio's struggle. Adama accompanied a delegation to visit the new ruler of the Sokoto Caliphate where dan Fodio presented Adama with a flag and then gave Adama his blessings to carry out the struggle in Fumbina. Adama raised an army and conquered all of the states in Fumbina, until he had the region under his command. He named the empire Adamawa after himself. Upon Adama's death in 1847, his son Muḥammadu Lawal became the ruler of Adamawa.[9]

Al-Ḥajj 'Umar Tall

Al-Ḥajj 'Umar ibn Sa'īd Tall (d. 1864) was a West African political leader, scholar, and military commander who founded the Tokolar empire. Al-Ḥajj 'Umar was born in the Futa Toro near the town of Podar on the Senegal River. 'Umar studied under the tutelage of his father and some of the prominent West African scholars of the Tijaniyyah brotherhood. 'Umar preached and proselytised in the Futa Jallon, where he acquired a substantial number of loyal supporters. His adherents were so numerous, well-armed, and well-financed that 'Umar's power became a serious threat to the traditional rulers of the Futa Jallon. In 1849, 'Umar was forced to move to the town of Dinguiray near the headwaters of the Niger River. During the next decade, 'Umar's troops conquered the lands stretching between the headwaters of the Niger and Timbuktu, creating a unified Tokolar empire which dominated the Western Sudan. Before his death in 1864, 'Umar was able to unite his followers into a formidable Islamic military and political force which dominated the Western Sudan for two decades until it was conquered by the French towards the end of the nineteenth century.[10]

---

9 See Robin Walker, 2005, *When We Ruled.*

10 See Robin Walker, 2005, *When We Ruled.*

15

Warriors and Martyrs

Ṭāriq ibn Ziyād

Ṭāriq ibn Ziyād (d. 720) was a former Berber slave who later became the heroic Muslim general who led the opening of Visigothic Hispania to Islam in 711. Mūsā ibn Nuṣayr, the Umayyad governor of North Africa, sent Ṭāriq in his place to govern Tangier. At this time, the Iberian Peninsula was under Visigoth rule but was rent by civil war. The heirs of King Witiza appealed to the Muslims for help. The Muslims quickly responded and sent Ṭāriq ibn Ziyād along with seven thousand men. After landing on the coastal strip overlooking the rock, which was later named The Rock of Ṭāriq, *Jabal Ṭāriq* (Gibraltar), Ṭāriq ordered his men to burn their ships. Ṭāriq rallied his troops with an inspirational speech, "Brothers in Islam! We now have the enemy in front of us and the deep sea behind us. We cannot return to our homes, because we have burnt our boats. We shall now either defeat the enemy and be victorious or we will die a coward's death by drowning in the sea. Who will follow me in battle?" Despite being outnumbered the Muslims swept through Andalusia and conquered the Iberian Peninsula. Ṭāriq was eventually re-called to Damascus by the Umayyad Caliph, Al-Walīd ibn 'Abd al-Malik, where he spent the rest of his life.[1]

---

[1] See Al-Maqqarī, 2006, *Breath of Perfumes.*

ʻAbdullāh ibn Yāsīn

ʻAbdullāh ibn Yāsīn (d. 1059) was the spiritual leader and founder of the Almoravid (*al-Murābiṭūn*) movement of North Africa and the Iberian Peninsula. Ibn Yāsīn was from Gazula, and a member of the Berber Ṣanhājah tribe. A stern disciplinarian and jurist of the Mālikī school of law, in 1046 Ibn Yāsīn was invited by the Judala ruler, Yaḥyā ibn Ibrāhīm, to promulgate the orthodox teachings of Islam to the Bedouin Berbers of the Western Sahara.[2] After a revolt of the Judala, Ibn Yāsīn was forced to withdraw to the south with his followers. In alliance with Yaḥyā ibn ʻUmar, the leader of the Lamtuna tribe, Ibn Yāsīn managed to quell the rebellion of the Bedouins. Rather than give up un-Islamic practices, the Berbers denounced Ibn Yāsīn and his teaching orthodoxy. Discouraged by this, Ibn Yāsīn withdrew with a small group of his loyal followers to Senegal. There he established a *ribāṭ* (ʻmonastery-fortressʼ), whose inhabitants (*Murābiṭūn*) gave their lives to worship, study and establishment of the *dīn*. This combination of devotion and military discipline along with communal life directed from the *ribāṭ* was noteworthy for its success. In spite of the fact that the rules which Ibn Yāsīn imposed on his followers were strict and the corporal punishment, which he personally inflicted for infractions, severe, his adherents soon numbered in the thousands, enough to subdue those very Berbers who had rejected his teachings. Expansion continued in subsequent years into the cities of Southern and Central Morocco. Before his death, Ibn Yāsīn created a base for the military expansion of Almoravid rule into North Africa and the Iberian Peninsula and laid down the guidelines by which it was to be governed. In 1059, Ibn Yāsīn died as a martyr while attempting to subjugate the Bargawata on the Atlantic coast.[3]

---

2 Despite being Muslims, many of the Ṣanhājah Berbers still clung to many heathen practices.

3 See Michael Brett, 1997, *The Berbers*.

Aḥmad ibn Ibrahīm al-Ghāzī

Aḥmad ibn Ibrāhīm al-Ghāzī (d. 1543), nicknamed the left-handed, was the courageous, charismatic Somali general of Adal. In the history of conflict in Africa and beyond, few stories equal the spectacular victories of Imam Aḥmad's opening of the Christian kingdom of Ethiopia to Islam. Imam Aḥmad brought three-quarters of Ethiopia under his governance during the Ethiopian-Adal War from 1529-43. This had immense consequences for the Horn of Africa. These included the conversion of a vast part of the Ethiopian population to Islam, the virtual collapse of the traditional Christian Ethiopian Empire and the export to Arabia of considerable quantities of gold. Imam Aḥmad was eventually martyred in 1543, after which the Adal state declined, and thereafter adopted a largely defensive stance.[4]

Lalla Fadhma N'Soumer

Lalla Fadhma N'Soumer[5] (d. 1863) was a courageous Berber heroine of the Kabyle *jihād* during the French conquest of Algiers. N'Soumer was only sixteen years old when the French invaded Kabyle. During this battle, N'Soumer headed the Algerian troops after the killing of the Algerian leader, Muḥammad al-Amdjed. N'Soumer took control and led her people to victory, a victory that was heralded throughout Kabylia. Even after the fall of Azazga and the ferocious repression by French troops, she mobilised the population and led them in more battles. She called her people to fight for Islam, their land and freedom. Her strong personality had a great influence on all of Kabylia, shown by the sacrifice and determination of the people during all the battles, especially those of Icherridene and Tachkrit, where the enemy troops were defeated decisively. The French finally asked for a ceasefire,

---

4 See Ṣihāb ad-Din, 2003, *Futūh al-Habashah: The Conquest of Abyssinia.*

5 *Lalla* is an honorific title reserved for women of high rank, or who are venerated as saints. *Lalla* is the female equivalent of *Sidi* (master). *Fadhma* is the Berber pronunciation of the Arabic name Fāṭimah.

which was accepted by N'Soumer, as a political and strategic military decision. She planned to use the period of the ceasefire to improve the land and reinforce her troops. The fields were ploughed and sowed, and arms factories were installed in all corners of the region. After three years, in 1857, the French broke the ceasefire after having prepared their armies and launched offensives against several large Algerian cities which were, until then, difficult to overtake. Fadhma N'Soumer died in 1863. She was thirty-three years old.[6]

'Abd al-Qādir al-Jazā'irī

'Abd al-Qādir al-Jazā'irī (d. 1883) was a Berber scholar, Sufi and military leader who led a war against the French invasion in the mid-nineteenth century. Al-Jazā'irī was born near the town of Mascara near Oran. In his childhood Al-Jazā'irī memorised the Qur'ān and was well trained in horsemanship, *tawḥīd* and philology. In 1825, he set out for the pilgrimage (*ḥajj*) to Makkah with his father. He returned to his homeland a few months before the arrival of the French. Throughout the subsequent period, Al-Jazā'irī demonstrated political and military leadership, and acted as a capable administrator and a persuasive orator. The large French armies brutally suppressed the native population. Al-Jazā'irī's failure to get support from eastern tribes, apart from the Berbers of Western Kabylia, also contributed to the quelling of the rebellion. After being denied refuge in Morocco in 1847, Al-Jazā'irī was ultimately forced to surrender to the French. He died in Damascus in 1883 where the French had allowed him to live in exile.[7]

Samory Toure

Samory Toure (d. 1900) was the founder of the Wassoulou Empire, an Islamic polity that resisted French rule in West Africa from 1882 until

6 Bewley, 2004, p. 103.

7 See 'Abd al-Razzāq bin al-Sab, 2000, *al-Amir 'Abd al-Qādir al-Jazā'iri wa adabuh.*

his capture in 1898. Born in South-Eastern Guinea, Toure converted to Islam early in his life. In 1848, Samory's mother was captured in the course of war by Séré-Burlay of the Cissé clan. After arranging his mother's freedom, Samory engaged himself to the service of the Cissés where he learned to handle weapons. He then joined the Bérété army, the enemies of the Cissé, for two years before rejoining his people, the Kamara. Named Kélétigui (war chief) in 1861, Samory took an oath to protect his people against both the Bérété and the Cissé. He created a professional army and placed close relations, notably his brothers and childhood friends, in positions of command. By 1867, Samory was a full-fledged war chief, with an army of his own centred on Sanankoro in the Guinea Highlands. Samory understood that he needed to accomplish two things: to create an efficient, loyal fighting force equipped with modern firearms, and to build a stable polity of his own. The French began to expand aggressively in West Africa in the late 1870s. In 1881, after numerous struggles, Samory was able to secure control of the key Dyula trading centre of Kankan, on the upper Milo River. In February 1882, a French expedition attacked one of Samory's armies besieging Keniera. Samory and his army were able to drive the French off for a number of years before his capture in 1898. Samory was exiled to Gabon where he died in captivity in 1900, following a bout of pneumonia.[8]

Muḥammad 'Abdullāh al-Ḥasan

Sayyid Muḥammad 'Abdullāh al-Ḥasan (d. 1920) was born in Northern Somaliland. At an early age, he travelled to Arabia in search of religious knowledge. His reputation for learning and his abilities as a teacher soon earned him the honorary title of *sayyid* (master). After studying the traditional Islamic sciences, Al-Ḥasan returned to Somalia in 1896, where he began to exhort his people to return to the

[8] See Robin Walker, 2005, *When We Ruled.*

orthodox teachings of Islam and where he founded the Dervish state. Sayyid al-Ḥasan was a politico-religious leader and master of oratory. He excelled in the art of composing impromptu poems that inspired his people to defend their land and faith. Al-Ḥasan led the struggle for over twenty years against European and Ethiopian imperialism in Somaliland. The Dervish state remained the only independent Muslim power in the African continent throughout the First World War. After a quarter of a century of holding the British at bay, the Dervishes were finally defeated in 1920, when the British government organised a combined air, sea, and land attack on them. Further attacks forced Al-Ḥasan's dwindling forces into Eastern Ethiopia, where he eventually succumbed to an attack of influenza and died in 1920.[9]

Macolm X (El-Ḥajj Malik el-Shabazz)

Malcolm X (d. 1965) has been described as one of the greatest and most influential African-Americans in recent history. He is credited with raising the self-esteem of thousands of African-Americans and reconnecting them with their African and Islamic heritage. Born Malcolm Little in Omaha in 1925, El-Ḥajj Malik el-Shabazz, commonly known as Malcolm X, was a charismatic civil rights leader and public speaker. The son of a Baptist preacher, at an early age Malcolm moved to Lansing, Michigan, with his parents, both of whom were lost to him in childhood. His father was murdered by the Klu Klux Klan and his mother had been committed to a mental hospital. After living in a series of foster homes, Malcolm X became involved in the criminal underworld of New York. In 1946, Malcolm was sentenced to ten years imprisonment for larceny. While in prison, Malcolm X joined Elijah Muḥammad's pseudo-Islamic group, the Nation of Islam. Paroled in 1952, Malcolm became an outspoken defender of the Nation of Islam's

---

9 See Abdi Sheik-Abdi, 1992, *Divine Madness: Mohammed Abdulle Hassan of Somalia (1856-1920).*

doctrines and, unlike Elijah Muḥammad, he received considerable publicity. For nearly a dozen years, he was the public face of the Nation of Islam. After revelations surfaced regarding Elijah Muḥammad's marital infidelity, Malcolm left the organisation after initially being suspended by Elijah Muḥammad. Soon after, Malcolm embraced Islam. Malcolm made the pilgrimage to Makkah in 1964 and renounced the racism he had preached whilst a follower of Elijah Muḥammad. On his pilgrimage, Malcolm witnessed the "sincere hospitality and overwhelming spirit of true brotherhood" from people of all colours and races in the Sacred Land of Makkah. Malcolm felt that Islam is the only religion that can solve the problem of racism, because believing in and submitting to the One God, removes racist attitudes from the human mind. Less than a year after becoming a Muslim, Malcolm was assassinated whilst giving a speech about African-American unity in New York. He died as a martyr of Islam.[10]

[10] See Malcolm X and Alex Haley, 1965, *The Autobiography of Malcolm X.*

Conclusion – The Superiority of *Taqwā*

Islam is uncompromising in its insistence on the equality of all believers before Allah. In the sight of Allah, human differences in society and affluence are irrelevant. Regardless of race, wealth or social status, all human beings are equally capable of attaining salvation in the Hereafter.[1] Allah looks at the hearts and deeds of His creatures and judges them accordingly. *Taqwā* resides in the heart, and is what distinguishes human beings in Islam. The word *taqwā* in Arabic conveys many meanings, linguistically it means 'to protect oneself', 'to take precaution', 'to ward off'. In the technical sense to have *taqwā* of Allah is to be conscious of Him, to fear Him and to be dutiful towards Him and to avoid disobeying Him and to discharge the obligations in obedience to Him. In pre-Islamic times, the Arabs were a proud people who believed in the inherent superiority of their tribes and forefathers. For the Arabs, merit (*faḍl*) and nobility (*karam*) meant ostentation and generosity. Islam radically altered this understanding by giving merit and nobility a new definition, *taqwā*, one that every Muslim strives for. The Qur'ānic verse in chapter 49

[1] Marlow, 1997, p. xi.

verse 13 informs us of the superiority of *taqwā* above everything else in the sight of Allah; *"Mankind! We created you from a male and female, and made you into peoples (shu'ūb) and tribes (qabā'il) so that you might come to know each other. The noblest among you in Allah's sight is the one with the most taqwā. Allah is All-Knowing, All-Aware."*[2]

Commenting on the aforementioned verse, Dr. Wahbah az-Zuḥaylī says *"Mankind!"* refers to all human beings irrespective of race, religion or gender.[3] Al-Baghawī says the *"male"* and *"female"* refer to Adam and Eve. "The verse informs us that human beings are equal in their lineage (because they are all descendants of the same father and mother)." Al-Baghawī continues, "It is said that the peoples (*shu'ūb*) refer to the non-Arabs, while the tribes (*qabā'il*) refers to the Arabs."[4] Interpreting the words, *"that you might come to know each other,"* Ibn al-Jawzī says, "It means that people should become acquainted with one another and not despise each other."[5] Aṭ-Ṭabarī says, "The noblest among you in the sight of your Lord is he who is most zealous in the fulfilment of the commands of Allah and in the avoidance of wrong actions against Him, and not he whose family is greatest or whose kinsfolk are the most numerous." Ibn Kathīr says regarding the *āyah* that, "All people are equal in their nobility in terms of their kinship in clay with Adam and Eve; they only differ in excellence (*faḍl*) in matters of the *dīn*, that is in obedience to Allah and in following His Prophet ﷺ." Ibn Kathīr continues, "People differ in excellence in the sight of Allah only in *taqwā* and not in their inherited merit (*aḥsāb*)." [Qāḍī Abū Bakr] Ibn al-'Arabī says, "In this verse, Allah defines honour and explains for us its reality." "The noblest among you in the sight of Allah is the one with the most *taqwā* not the noblest in lineage," Az-Zamakhsharī adds.[6] As-

2 Sūrat al-Ḥujurāt 49:13.
3 Az-Zuḥaylī, 2005, vol. 13, p. 590.
4 Al-Baghawī, 2002, p. 1224.
5 Ibn al-Jawzī, 2002, pp. 1332-1336.
6 Az-Zamakhsharī, 2005, p. 1041.

Suyūṭī says, "Pride and boasting is in *taqwā* alone."[7] Al-Bayḍāwī adds, "There is no place for pride in one's lineage. It is (*taqwā*) by which souls become perfect and by which individuals differ in excellence. Therefore whoever desires nobility, let him seek it in *taqwā*."[8] As-Sa'dī says, "The one with the most *taqwā* in the sight of Allah is the one who is most obedient and far away from transgressions, not the one who has the strongest tribe or most honourable lineage! Indeed, Allah the Exalted is All-Powerful and Fully-Aware. He knows those who have *taqwā* outwardly and inwardly. There are amongst mankind people who have *taqwā* outwardly but not inwardly. Allah rewards each person according to what he deserves."[9] Al-Baghawī says, "Allah concludes the *āyah* by stating that the most exalted of people in rank in the sight of Allah are the ones with the most *taqwā*."[10] Commenting on the conclusion of the verse, Az-Zuhaylī says, "Allah possesses full knowledge of everyone and everything. He is fully aware of everyone's internal states and thoughts."[11] Ash-Shinqīṭī says, "This Qur'ānic *āyah* indicates that the religion of Islam is an authentic heavenly *dīn*. Islam does not look at an individual's complexion, ethnicity or form. Indeed what is recognised in the *dīn* is a person's moral conduct and obedience towards Allah, the Great and Majestic. Truly, the noblest person and the best amongst mankind is the one with the most *taqwā*. An impious person has no honour or superiority, even if he is a descendent of a noble lineage.[12]

---

[7] As-Suyūṭī, 2004, p. 517.
[8] Al-Bayḍāwī, 2001, p. 1002.
[9] As-Sa'dī, 2003, p. 767.
[10] Al-Baghawī, 2002, p. 1224.
[11] Az-Zuḥaylī, 2005, vol. 13, p. 590.
[12] Ash-Shinqīṭī, 2003, p. 1650.

Bibliography

Arabic Sources

'Abd al-Ghaffār, Fu'ād ibn Sirāj. *Sīrah zawjāt ar-rasūl fī ad-dunyā wa'l-ākhirah.* Cairo: Al-Tawfikia Bookshop, 2003.

'Abd al-Ḥalīm, Rajab Muḥammad. *Al-'urūbah wa'l-Islām fī Ifrīqiyyah ash-sharqiyyah min ẓuhūr al-Islām ilā qudūm al-Burtughāliyyīn.* Cairo: Dār al-Nahḍah al-'Arabiyyah, 1999.

'Abd al-Qādir, at-Tījānī and aṭ-Ṭayyib, Muddaththir 'Abd ar-Raḥīm (ed.). *Al-Islām fī Ifrīqiyyah.* Beirut: Dār al-Fikr, 2001.

Abū Bakr, 'Alī ash-Shaykh Aḥmad. *Ma'ālim al-hijratayn ilā al-Ḥabasha.* Riyadh: Maktabah al-Tawbah, 1993.

ad-Dimashqī, Shams ad-Dīn, Muḥammad. *Nukhbat al-dahr fī 'ajā'ib al-barr wa al-baḥr,* Leipzig, 1923.

Aḥmad al-'Alī, Ṣāliḥ. 'Alī ibn Muḥammad. *Sāḥib az-Zinj.* Beirut: Dār al-Midār al-Islāmī, 2006.

al-Aṣfahānī, al-Ḥusayn ibn Muḥammad. *Mu'jam mufradāt alfāẓ al-Qur'ān.* Beirut: Dār al-Fikr, 2009.

al-Baghawī, Abū Muḥammad al-Ḥusayn. *Tafsīr al-Baghawī: Ma'ālim at-tanzīl.* Beirut: Dār Ibn Ḥazm, 2002.

al-Bayḍāwī, Abū Muḥammad ibn 'Umar. *Anwār at-tanzīl wa asrār al-ta'wīl.* Beirut: Dār Sader, 2001.

al-Bayhaqī, Aḥmad ibn al-Ḥusayn. *As-sunan al-kubrā.* Beirut: Dār al-Kutub al-'Ilmiyyah, 1994.

al-Bukhārī, Muḥammad ibn Ismā'īl. *Ṣaḥīḥ al-Bukhārī.* Beirut: Al-Maktabah al-'Aṣriyyah, 2005.

adh-Dhahabī, Muḥammad ibn Aḥmad. *Siyar a'lām an-nubalā.* Beirut: Mu'assasat ar-Risalah, 1988.

adh-Dhahabī, Muḥammad Ḥusayn. *al-Isrā'īliyyāt fī at-tafsīr wa'l-Ḥadīth.* Cairo: Maktabah Wahbah, 2004.

al-Fāris, Abū al-Ḥusayn Aḥmad. *Maqāyis al-lughah.* Beirut: Dār al-Kutub al-'Ilmiyyah, 1999.

al-Fayrūzābādī, Muḥammad ibn Ya'qūb. *Al-qāmūs al-muḥīṭ.* Beirut: Al-Maktabah al-'Aṣriyyah, 2009.

al-Fulānī, aṭ-Ṭayyib 'Abd ar-Raḥīm, Muḥammad. *Al-falātah fī Ifrīqiyyah.* Kuwait City: Dār al-Kitāb al-Ḥadīth, 1994.

al-Gharyānī, al-Ṣādiq 'Abd ar-Raḥman, *Mudawwanah al-fiqh al-Mālikī wa adilatihi* vol. 2, Beirut: Musasah al-Riyyān, 2002.

al-Ḥajūrī, Abū Bashīr Muḥammad ibn 'Alī az-Za'karī. *Al-qawl al-ḥasan fī faḍā'il ahl al-Yaman.* Cairo: Dār al-Athār, 2007.

al-Ḥākim, Abū 'Abdullāh. *Al-Mustadrak 'alā aṣ-ṣaḥīḥayn.* Beirut: Dār Ibn Ḥazm, 2007.

al-Hāshimī, 'Abd al-Mun'im. *Ahl as-sayf wa'l-qalam.* Beirut: Dār al-Ibn Kathīr, 1993.

al-'Imādī, Abū Su'ūd. *Irshād al-'aql as-sālim ilā mazāyā al-kitāb al-karīm.* Beirut: Dār al-Kutub al-'Ilmiyyah, 1999.

al-Iṣṭakhrī, Abū Ishāq Ibrāhīm ibn Muḥammad. *Al-masālik wa'l-mamālik.* Leiden: Brill, 1870.

al-Jāḥiẓ, Abū 'Uthmān 'Amr. "*Kitāb fakhr as-sūdān 'alā al-bīḍān.*" In *Rasā'il al-Jāḥiẓ, Volume 1*, by 'Abd as-Salām Muḥammad Hārūn (ed.), 173-226. Cairo: [Publisher name unknown], 1960.

——. *Rasā'il al-Jāḥiẓ vol. 1.* Beirut: Dār al-Kutub al-'Ilmiyyah, 2000.

al-Kandahlāwī, Muḥammad Yūsuf. *Ḥayāt aṣ-ṣaḥābah.* Cairo: Al-Maktabah al-Qawmiyyah, 2005.

al-Kisā'ī, Abū 'Abd ar-Raḥmān. *Qaṣaṣ wa mawālid al-anbiyā'.* Beirut: Dār al-Kutub al-'Ilmiyyah, 2004.

al-Maqdiṣī, Muṭahhar ibn Ṭāhir. *Kitāb al-bad' wa't-tārīkh.* Paris: Ernest Leroux, 1903.

al-Mas'ūdī, Abū al-Ḥasan ibn 'Alī ibn al-Ḥusayn. *Murūj adh-dhahab.* Beirut: Université Libanaise, 1966.

al-Mubārakfūrī, Ṣafī ar-Raḥmān. *Ar-raḥīq al-makhtūm.* Jeddah: Dār al-Minhāj, 2005.

al-Muttaqī, 'Alā ad-Dīn 'Alī ibn Ḥusām ad-Dīn. *Kanz al-'ummāl, 8 parts.* Hyderabad: Dā'irat al-Ma'ārif, 1895.

al-Naḥawī, al-Khalīl. *Ifrīqiyyah al-muslimah.* Beirut: Dār al-Gharb al-Islāmī, 1993.

an-Nasā'i, Abū 'Abd ar-Raḥmān Aḥmad ibn Shu'ayb. *Sunan an-Nasā'i.* Riyadh: Dār as-Salām, 1999.

an-Nāṣirī, Aḥmad ibn Khālid. *Kitāb al-istiqsā' lī akhbār duwal al-maghrib al-aqṣā.* Casablanca: [Publisher name unknown], 1955.

al-Qarāfī, Abū al-'Abbās Aḥmad. *Al-Dhakhīrah* vol. 4. Beirut: Dār al-Kutub al-'Ilmiyyah, 2008.

al-Qurṭubī, Abū 'Abdullāh Muḥammad. *Jāmi' aḥkām al-Qur'ān.* Beirut: Al-Maktabah al-'Aṣriyyah, 2009.

ar-Rabī', Abū al-Ḥasan. *Faḍā'il ash-Shām wa Dimashq.* Damascus: Al-Mujma' al-'Ilmī, 1950.

ar-Rāzī, Muḥammad ibn Abū Bakr ibn 'Abd al-Qādir. *Mukhtār aṣ-Ṣiḥāḥ.* Beirut: Dār El-Marefah, 2005.

as-Sa'dī, 'Abd ar-Raḥmān. *Taysīr al-karīm ar-raḥmān fī tafsīr kalām al-mannān.* Beirut: Dār Ibn Ḥazm, 2003.

as-Sa'dī, Abd ar-Raḥmān ibn 'Abdullāh ibn 'Imrān ibn 'Āmir. *Tārīkh as-Sūdān.* Paris: E. Leroux, 1900.

as-Sanūsī, Muṣṭafā Zooglool. *Azhār ar-rubā fī bilād Yurūbā.* Lagos: Dār ad-Da'wat wa'l-Irshād, 1987.

aṣ-Ṣalābī, 'Alī Muḥammad. *Ḥarakah al-fatḥ al-Islāmī fī ash-Shimāl al-Ifrīqī.* Mansurah: Dār al-Wafā, 2003.

as-Sarjānī, Rāghib. *Al-mawsū'ah al-musirah fī at-tārīkh al-Islāmī.* Cairo: Iqraa Kotob, 2005.

ash-Shaqafah, Muḥammad Bashīr. *Al-fiqh al-Mālikī fī thawbih al-jadīd vol. 3.* Damascus: Dār al-Qalam, 2007.

ash-Shāṭibī, Abū Ishāq. *Al-muwāfaqāt fī uṣūl ash-sharī'ah.* Cairo: Dār al-Ḥadīth, 2006.

ash-Shinqīṭī, Muḥammad al-Amīn. *Aḍwā' al-bayān fī īḍāḥ al-Qur'ān bi'l-Qur'ān.* Beirut: Dār al-Kutub al-'Ilmiyyah, 2003.

as-Sijistānī, Abū Bakr 'Abdullāh ibn Abū Dāwūd. *Sunan Abū Dāwūd.* Riyadh: Dār as-Salām, 1999.

as-Suyūṭī, Abū Faḍl 'Abd ar-Raḥmān. *Raf' sha'n al-Ḥubshān.* Beirut: Dār al-Kutub al-'Ilmiyyah, 2004.

———. *Tafsīr ad-durr al-manthūr.* Beirut: Dār el-Fikr, 2009.

———. *Jam' al-Jawāmi'* or *al-Jāmi' al-Kabīr.* Mawqi' Multaqā Ahl al-Ḥadīth (www.ahlalhadeeth.com).

aṭ-Ṭabarī, Abū Ja'far Muḥammad ibn Jarīr. *Jāmi' al-bayān fī ta'wīl al-Qur'ān.* Cairo: Dār al-Salām, 2007.

aṭ-Ṭabarī, Muḥammad ibn Jarīr. *Qaṣaṣ al-anbiyā'.* Beirut: Dār Ibn Ḥazm, 2008.

———. *Tārīkh aṭ-Ṭabarī.* Riyadh: International Ideas Home, 2008.

at-Tirmidhī, Abū 'Īsā Muḥammad ibn 'Īsā. *Jāmi' at-Tirmidhī.* Riyadh: Dār as-Salām, 1999.

al-'Umarī, Ibn Faḍl Allāh. *Masālik al-abṣār fi mamālik al-amṣār.* Al-'Ayn: Markaz Zāyid lil-Turāth wa at-Tārīkh, 2006.

al-Wāqidī, Muḥammad ibn 'Umar. *Kitāb al-maghāzī.* Beirut: World of Books, 2006.

al-Wazzān, al-Ḥasan ibn Muḥammad. *Waṣf Ifrīqiyyah.* Beirut: Dār al-Gharb al-Islāmī, 1983.

al-Ya'qūbī, Aḥmad ibn Abū Ya'qūb. *Kitāb al-buldān.* Leiden: Brill, 1892.

az-Zamakhsharī, Abū Qāsim Maḥmūd. *Tafsīr al-kashshāf.* Beirut: Dār El-Marefah, 2005.

az-Zuḥaylī, Wahbah. *At-tafsīr al-munīr fī al-'aqīdah wa'sh-sharī'ah wa'l-minhaj: vol. 13.* Damascus: Dār al-Fikr, 2005.

Badawī, ‘Abduh. *Ash-shu‘arā as-sūd wa-khaṣā’isuhum fī ash-shi‘r al-‘Arabī.* Cairo: Al-Hai’at al-Miṣrīyyat al-’Ammah lī al-Kitāb, 1973.

——. *as-sūd wa’l-ḥaḍārat al-‘Arabiyyah.* Cairo: [Publisher name unknown], 1976.

Bin al-Sab, ‘Abd al-Razzāq. *al-Amir ‘Abd al-Qādir al-Jazā‘iri wa adabuh.* Kuwait: Mu’assasat Jā’izat ‘Abd al-Aziz Su’ūd al-Bābṭīn, 2000.

Chelebi, Awliyā. *Ar-riḥlah ilā miṣr wa’s-sūdān wa’l-ḥabashah.* Cairo: Dār al-Afāq, 2005.

Ḥasan, Ibrāhīm Muḥammad. *Al-muslimūn fī al-ḥabashah.* Elharam: Ein for Human and Social Studies, 2009.

Ibn ‘Abd al-Barr, Abū ‘Umar Yūsuf. *Al-isti‘āb fī ma‘rifat al-aṣḥāb.* Beirut: Dār al-Kutub al-‘Ilmiyyah, 1995.

——. *Al-kāfī fī fiqh ahl al-Madīnah al-Mālikī.* Beirut: Al-Maktabah al-‘Aṣriyyah, 2007.

Ibn Abī Zayd al-Qayrawānī, ’Abū Muḥammad ‘Abdullāh. *Kitāb al-Jāmi’.* Beirut: Dar al-Gharb al-Islami, 1990.

Ibn al-‘Arabī, ’Abū Bakr Muḥammad. *Aḥkām al-Qur’ān.* Beirut: Dār al-Kitāb al-‘Arabī, 2009.

Ibn al-Athīr, ‘Alī ibn Muḥammad. *Al-kāmil fī at-tārīkh.* Riyadh: International Ideas Home, 2008.

——. *Usd al-ghābah fī ma‘rifat aṣ-Ṣaḥābah.* Beirut: Dār Iḥyā’ at-Turāth al-‘Arabī, 1970.

Ibn al-Faqīh, Abū Bakr Aḥmad ibn Ibrāhīm al-Hamadhānī. *Kitāb al-buldān.* Leiden: Brill, 1885.

Ibn al-Ḥajjāj, Muslim al-Qushayrī. *Ṣaḥīḥ Muslim.* Beirut: Dār Iḥyā’ at-Turāth al-‘Arabī, 2000.

Ibn al-Jalab, Abū Qāsim ‘Abdullāh ibn Ḥusayn. *At-tafrī‘.* Tunis: Dār al-Gharb al-Islāmī, 2008.

Ibn al-Jawzī, Abū Faraj ‘Abd ar-Raḥmān. *Kitāb al-mawḍū‘āt min al-aḥādīth al-marfū‘āt.* Beirut: Dār Ibn Hazm, 2008.

——. *Ṣifat aṣ-ṣafwah.* Beirut: Al-Maktabah al-‘Aṣriyyah, 2004.

———. *Tanwīr al-ghabash fī faḍl as-sūdān wa'l-ḥabash.* Riyadh: Dār ash-Sharīf, 1998.

———. *Zād al-maṣīr fī 'ilm at-tafsīr.* Beirut: Dār Ibn Ḥazm, 2002.

Ibn Anas, Mālik. *Al-Muwaṭṭa.* Cairo: Dār al-Ma'rifah, 2008.

Ibn Baṭṭūṭah, Muḥammad ibn Abū 'Abdullāh. *Riḥlah Ibn Baṭṭūṭah.* Beirut: Dār an-Nifā'is, 2004.

Ibn Ḥajar al-'Asqalānī, Aḥmad ibn 'Alī. *Fatḥ al-bārī bi sharḥ Ṣaḥīḥ al-Bukhārī.* Riyadh: International Ideas Home, 2008.

———. *Al-iṣābah fī tamyīz aṣ-Ṣaḥābah.* Beirut: Dār al-Kutub al-'Ilmiyyah, 1995.

Ibn Ḥanbal, Aḥmad ibn Muḥammad. *Musnad al-Imām Aḥmad ibn Ḥanbal.* Beirut: 'Ālam al-Kutub, 1998.

Ibn Ḥibbān, Muḥammad. *Ṣaḥīḥ Ibn Ḥibbān.* Riyadh: International Ideas Home, 2008.

Ibn Hishām, Abū Muḥammad 'Abd al-Malik. *As-Sīrah an-nabawiyyah.* Beirut: Dār El-Marefah, 2006.

Ibn Kathīr, Abū al-Fidā Ismā'īl. *As-Sīrah an-nabawiyyah.* Cairo: Maktabat aṣ-Ṣafā, 2006.

———. *Qaṣaṣ al-anbiyā.* Cairo: Dār as-Salām, 2007.

———. *Tafsīr al-Qur'ān al-'aẓīm.* Beirut: Dār Ibn Ḥazm, 2000.

Ibn Khaldūn, 'Abd ar-Raḥmān ibn Muḥammad. *Muqaddimah Ibn Khaldūn.* Cairo: Dār al-Fajr, 2004.

———. *Tārīkh Ibn Khaldūn.* Beirut: Al-Maktabah al-'Aṣriyyah, 2009.

Ibn Mājah, Abū 'Abdullāh Muḥammad. *Sunan Ibn Mājah.* Riyadh: Dār as-Salām, 1999.

Ibn Manẓūr, Muḥammad ibn Mukarram. *Lisān al-'Arab: Volumes 1-5.* Cairo: Dār el-Hadith, 2003.

Ibn an-Nuḥās, Abū Zakariyyā Aḥmad ibn Ibrāhīm. *Mashārī' al-ashwāq ilā maṣārī' al-'ushshāq.* Beirut: Dār al-Bashā'ir al-Islāmiyyah, 2002.

Ibn Qayyim al-Jawziyyah, Muḥammad ibn Abū Bakr. *Aṭ-ṭibb al-nabawī.* Cairo: Maktabah ath-Thaqāfah ad-Dīniyyah, 2004.

Ibn Qayyim al-Jawziyyah, *Rawḍah al-muḥibbīn wa nuzhat al-mushtāqīn.* Cairo: Maktabah al-Raḥāb, 2007.

———. *Zād al-ma'ād fī hudā khayr al-'ibād.* Beirut: Dār El-Marefah, 2006.

Ibn Qutaybah, Abū Muḥammad 'Abdullāh ibn Muslim. *Kitāb al-ma'ārif.* Cairo: Ma'ārif, 1969.

Ibn Raslān, Abū 'Abdullāh Muḥammad ibn Sa'īd. *Faḍl al-'Arabiyyah wa wujūb ta'allumiha 'alā al-muslimīn.* Cairo: Dār al-'Ulūm al-Islāmiyyah, 1989.

Ibn Rustah, Abū 'Alī Aḥmad ibn 'Umar. *Kitāb al-a'lāq an-nafīsah.* Leiden: Brill, 1892.

Ibn Taymiyyah, Taqī ad-Dīn Aḥmad. *Iqtiḍā' aṣ-ṣirāṭ al-mustaqīm mukhālafah aṣḥāb al-jaḥīm.* Beirut: Dār al-Fikr, 2003.

———. *Manāqib ash-Shām wa ahlihi.* Beirut: Al-Maktabah al-Islāmiyyah, 1985.

———. *Sharh muqaddimah uṣūl at-tafsīr.* Beirut: Dār Ibn Ḥazm, 2006.

'Iyāḍ, al-Qāḍī. *Ash-shifā bi ta'rīf ḥuqūq al-muṣṭafā.* Cairo: Maktabah as-Ṣafā, 2002.

Jawwād, 'Alī Aḥmad. *Aḥkām al-asrā fī al-fiqh al-Islāmī wa'l-qānūn al-waḍ'ī.* Beirut: Dār El-Marefah, 2005.

Muḥammad, Nabīlah Ḥasan. *Fī tārīkh Afrīqiyyah al-Islāmiyyah.* Cairo: Dār al-Ma'rifah al-Jāmi'iyyah, 2008.

Murīdī, Abū Bakr Aḥmad. *Tārīkh al-anbiyā.* Beirut: Dār al-Kutub al-'Ilmiyyah, 2004.

Mūsā, 'Āyadah al-Gharab. *Tijārah al-'abīd fī Ifrīqiyyah.* Cairo: Maktabah ash-Shurūq ad-Dawliyyah, 2007.

Muṣṭafā, 'Alī ibn. *Mir'āt al-ḥubūsh fī al-uṣūl (Ms.).* London: British Museum, Department of Oriental Manuscripts and Printed Books, Or. 11226.

Nājī, 'Alī Ayyūb. *Lamaḥāt 'an al-Islām fī naygirīyā bayna al-ams wa'l-yawm.* Kuwait: Dār al-Kitāb al-Ḥadīth, 2000.

Pāshā, 'Abd ar-Raḥmān Ra'fat. *Ṣuwar min ḥayāt aṣ-ṣaḥābah.* Cairo: Islamic Literature House, 1997.

———. *Ṣuwar min ḥayāt at-tābi'īn.* Cairo: Islamic Literature House, 1997.

Shams ad-Dīn, Ibrāhīm. *Nawādir an-nisā fi kitāb al-mustaṭrif wa kutub at-turāth al-'Arabī.* Beirut: Dār al-Kutub al-'Ilmiyyah, 2002.

Ṭaqūsh, Muḥammad Suhayl. *Tārīkh al-'Arab qabl al-Islām.* Beirut: Dār an-Nifās, 2009.

Yūsuf, Ḥasan 'Abd al-Jalīl. *Al-adab al-jāḥilī.* Cairo: Al-Mukhtār, 2003.

Zanātī, Maḥmūd Salām. *Al-Islām wa't-taqālīd al-qibliyyah fī Ifrīqiyyah'.* Cairo: [Publisher name unknown], 1992.

English Sources

The Holy Bible with Apocrypha. Oxford: Oxford University Press, 1995

'Alī, 'Abdullah Yūsuf. *The Meaning of The Holy Qur'ān.* Maryland: Amana Corporation, 1992.

Adamu, Mahdi. *The Hausa Factor in West African History.* Zaria: Ahmadu Bello University Press, 1978.

Ahmad, K. J. *Hundred Great Muslims.* Chicago: Kazi Publications, 1987.

Ali, Maulana Muḥammad (translator). *The Holy Qur'ān.* Chicago: Speciality Promotions Co., 1985.

Ajayi, J. F. Ade and Crowder, Michael (ed.). *A History of West Africa.* London: Longmans, 1971.

al-Ashanti, 'Abdul-Haq ibn Kofi Kwesi. *Defining Legends - Analysis of Afrocentric Writings on Islaam.* London: Salafi Manhaj, 2004.

Alawiye, Imran Hamza. *Ibn Jawzi's Apologia on behalf of the Black People and their status in Islam: A Critical Edition and Translation of Kitāb Tanwīr al-Ghabash fī Faḍl as-Sūdān wa'l-Ḥabash.* London: University of London, 1985.

al-Ismail, Tahia. *The Life of Muḥammad (saas).* London: Ta-Ha Publishers, 2011.

al-Khayyaat, Abdul-Aziz, (translated by Khalifa Ezzat and Heather Shaw). *Human Rights and Racial Discrimination in Islam.* Cairo: Dar as-Salam, 2002.

al-Kisā'ī, Muḥammad ibn 'Abdullāh, (translated by Wheeler M. Thackston Jr.). *Tales of the Prophets (Qiṣaṣ al-anbiyā').* Chicago: Great Books of the Islamic World, Inc., 1997.

al-Makkari, Ahmed ibn Mohammed. *The History of the Mohammedan Dynasties in Spain.* London: Royal Asiatic Society Books, 2002.

al-Maqqarī, Aḥmad ibn Muḥammad, (translated by Charles Horne). *Breath of Perfumes.* Montana: Kessinger Publishing, 2006.

al-Qaraḍāwī, Yūsuf. *The Lawful and the Prohibited in Islam.* London: Al-Birr Foundation, 2003.

Arogundade, Ben. *Black Beauty.* London: Pavilion, 2000.

Austen, Ralph. *Trans-Saharan Africa in World History.* New York: Oxford University Press, 2010.

as-Sa'dī, 'Abd al-Rahmān ibn 'Abdullāh, (translated by John Hunwick). *Timbuktu and the Songhay Empire: As-Sa'di's Tārīkh as-Sūdān down to 1613, and other contemporary documents.* Leiden: Brill, 2003.

as-Suyūṭī, Jalāl ad-Dīn 'Abd ar-Raḥmān (translation edited by Ahmad Thomson). As-Suyūṭī's *Medicine of the Prophet.* London: Ta-Ha Publishers, 1994.

aṭ-Ṭabarī, (translated by David Waines). *The History of aṭ-Ṭabarī: Volume XXXVI: The Revolt of the Zanj: AD 869 – 879 / A.H. 255 – 265.* New York: State University of New York Press, 1992.

aṭ-Ṭabarī, (translated by Franz Rosenthal). *The History of aṭ-Ṭabarī: Volume I: General Introduction and From the Creation to the Flood.* New York: State University of New York Press, 1987.

aṭ-Ṭabarī, (translated by Philip M. Fields). *The History of aṭ-Ṭabarī: Volume XXXVII: The 'Abbāsid Recovery.* New York: State University of New York Press, 1987.

aṭ-Ṭabarī, (translated by William M. Brinner). *The History of aṭ-Ṭabarī: Volume II: Prophets and Patriarchs.* New York: State University of New York Press, 1987.

——. *The History of* aṭ-Ṭabarī*: Volume III: The Children of Israel.* New York: State University of New York Press, 1991.

at-Tabrīzī, Muḥammad ibn 'Abdullāh, (translated by James Robson). *Mishkāt al-Maṣābīḥ.* Lahore: Sh. Muḥammad Ashraf, 2006.

ath-Tha'labī, Abū Isḥāq Aḥmad ibn Muḥammad ibn Ibrāhīm, (translated by William M. Brinner). *'Arā'is al-Majālis fī Qiṣaṣ al-Anbiyā or 'Lives of the Prophets'.* Leiden: Brill, 2002.

Austin, Allan D. *African Muslims in Antebellum America.* London: Routledge, 1997.

Azumah, John Alembillah. *The Legacy of Arab-Islam in Africa: A Quest for Inter-religious Dialogue.* Oxford: Oneworld Publications, 2001.

Bābā at-Tinbuktī, Aḥmad (translated by John Hunwick and Fatima Harrak). *Mi'rāj aṣ-Ṣu'ūd: Aḥmad Bābā's Replies on Ethnicity and Slavery.* Rabat: Institut des Etudes Africaines [Université Mohamed V], 2000.

Berry, Tariq. *The Unknown Arabs.* [Place of publication unknown]: Tariq Berry, 2001.

Bewley, Aisha, *Muslim Women - A Biographical Dictionary.* London: Ta-Ha Publishers, 2004.

Blankinship, Khalid Yahya. *The End of the Jihād State: The reign of Hishām ibn 'Abd al-Malik and the collapse of the Umayyads.* Albany: State University of New York Press, 1994.

Blyden, Edward Wilmot. *Christianity, Islam and the Negro Race.* Baltimore: Black Classic Press, 1994.

Boahen, A. Adu. *Africa Under Colonial Domination 1880-1935.* Berkeley: University of California Press, 1990.

———. *African Perspective on Colonialism.* Baltimore: The Johns Hopkins University Press, 1989.

Boyd, Jean and Mack, Beverly B. [ed.]. *Collected Works of Nana Asma'u, Daughter of Usman dan Fodiyo (1793 - 1864).* East Lansing: Michigan State University Press, 1984.

Brett, Michael. *The Berbers.* Oxford: Blackwell Publishers, 1997.

Clarence-Smith, William Gervase. *Islam and the Abolition of Slavery.* New York: Oxford University Press, 2006.

Clarke, John Henrik (Ed.). *Malcolm X - The Man and His Times.* New Jersey: Africa World Press, 1990.

Clarke, Peter B. *West Africa and Islam: A Study of Religious Development from the 8th to the 20th Century.* London: Edward Arnold, 1982.

Colville, Jim (translator). *Sobriety and Mirth: A Selection of the Shorter Writings of al-Jāḥiẓ.* London: Keegan Paul, 2002.

Dannin, Robert. *Black Pilgrimage to Islam.* Oxford: Oxford University Press, 2002.

Danziger, Raphael. *Abd el Qadir and the Algerians: Resistance to the French and Internal Consolidation.* New York: Homes & Meier, 1977.

Davidson, Basil. *Africa in History.* New York: Simon & Schuster, 1995.

——. *West Africa before the Colonial Era, A History to 1850.* London: Longman, 1998.

Diop, Cheikh Anta, (translated by Harold Salemson). *Precolonial Black Africa.* Chicago: Lawrence Hill Books, 1987.

Diop, Cheikh Anta, (translated by Mercer Cook). *The African Origin of Civilization: Myth or Reality.* Chicago: Lawrence Hill Books, 1974.

Diop, Cheikh Anta, (translated by Yaa-Lengi Meema Ngemi). *Civilization or Barbarism: An Authentic Anthropology.* New York: Lawrence Hill Books, 1991.

Diouf, Sylviane A. *Servants of Allah: African Muslims Enslaved in the Americas.* New York: New York University Press, 1998.

Doi, ʻAbdur Rahman I. *Woman in Shariʻah (Islamic Law).* London: Ta-Ha Publishers, 1996.

Doi, Abdur Rahman I. *Islam in Nigeria.* Zaria: Gaskiya Corporation Ltd., 1984.

Du Bois, W.E.B. *The Souls of Black Folk.* New York: Bantam Books, 1989.

Faisal, Abdullah. *100 Fabricated Hadith.* London: Darul Islam Publishers, 2000.

Frost, Peter. *Fair Women, Dark Men: The Forgotten Roots of Color Prejudice.* Christchurch: Cybereditions, 2005.

Gabriel, Deborah. *Layers of Blackness: Colourism in the African Diaspora.* London: Imani Media Ltd, 2007.

Gbadamosi, T. G. O. *The Growth of Islam among the Yoruba, 1841-1908.* London: Longman, 1978.

Gibb, H. A. R. *Studies on the Civilization of Islam.* Oxford: Routledge, 2007.

Glazier, Stephen P. (ed.). *Encyclopedia of African and African-American Religions.* New York: Routledge, 2001.

Goldenberg, David M. *The Curse of Ham: Race and Slavery in Early Judaism, Christianity and Islam.* Princeton, New Jersey: Princeton University Press, 2003.

Goldziher, Ignaz, (translated by C.R. Barber and S. M. Stren). *Muslim Studies.* New Jersey: Transaction Publishers, 2009.

Gomez, Michael A. *Black Crescent: The Experience and Legacy of African Muslims in the Americas.* New York: Cambridge University Press, 2005.

Hardy, Paul. *Islam and the Race Question.* Cambridge: The Muslim Academic Trust, 2002.

Houtsma, M. Th. And van Donzel, E. [Ed.] *E. J. Brill's First Encyclopaedia of Islam 1913-1936.* Leiden: Brill, 1993.

Hunter, Margaret L. *Race, Gender, and the Politics of Skin Tone.* New York: Routledge, 2005.

Hunwick, John and Powell, Eve Troutt. *The African Diaspora in the Mediterranean Lands of Islam.* Princeton, NJ: Markus Wiener Publishers, 2007.

Hunwick, John. *Timbuktu & the Songhay Empire.* Leiden: Brill, 2003.

———. *West Africa, Islam and the Arab World.* NJ: Markus Wiener Publishers, 2006.

Ibn Abī Zayd al-Qayrawānī, (translated by Abdassamad Clarke). *A Madinan View on the Sunnah, Courtesy, Wisdom, Battles and History [=translation of Kitāb al-Jāmiʿ].* London: Ta-Ha Publishers, 1999.

Ibn an-Naqīb, Aḥmad ibn Lu'lu', (translated by Nu Ha Mim Keller). *'Umdat as-sālik wa 'uddat an-nāsik (Reliance of the Traveller: a classic manual of Islamic sacred law).* Maryland: Amana Publications, 2008.

Ibn Baṭṭūṭah, Abū 'Abdullāh, (edited by Tim Mackintosh-Smith). *The Travels of Ibn Baṭṭūṭah.* London: Picador, 2002.

Ibn Ḥazm, Abū Muḥammad 'Alī, (translated by Anthony Arberry). *The Ring of the Dove.* London: Luzac Oriental, 1994.

Ibn Isḥāq, (translated by Guillaume, Alfred). *The Life of Muḥammad: A Translation of Sīrat Rasūl Allāh.* Karachi: Oxford University Press, 2007.

Ibn Khaldūn, (translated by Franz Rosenthal). *The Muqaddimah: An Introduction to History.* Princeton, NJ: Princeton University Press, 2nd edn., 2005.

Ibn Qayyim al-Jawziyyah, Shams ad-Dīn, (translated by Penelope Johnstone). *Medicine of the Prophet.* Cambridge: The Islamic Texts Society, 2008.

Ibn Qayyim, al-Jawziyyah, (translated by Jalal Abual Rub). *Healing with the Medicine of the Prophet.* London: Darussalam, 2003.

Ibn Rajab al-Ḥanbalī, (translated by Abdassamad Clarke). *The Compendium of Knowledge and Wisdom.* London: Turath Publishing, 2007.

Isaac, Benjamin. *The Invention of Racism in Classical Antiquity.* Princeton, New Jersey: Princeton University Press, 2004.

'Iyāḍ, al-Qāḍī, (translated by Aisha Abdarrahman Bewley). *Muḥammad the Messenger of Allah: Ash-Shifā of Qāḍī 'Iyāḍ.* Cape Town: *Madīnah* Press, 2006.

Jackson, Sherman A. *Islam and the Black American.* New York: Oxford University Press, 2005.

——. *Islam and the Problem of Black Suffering.* New York: Oxford University Press, 2009.

——. *Islamic Law and the State: The Constitutional Jurisprudence of Shihāb ad-Dīn al-Qarāfī.* Leiden: Brill, 1996.

Johnson, Samuel. *The History of the Yorubas.* Lagos: CSS Limited, 1921.

Kamara, M. Ibrahim and McEwan (ed). *Biographies of the Rightly Guided Caliphs: Prepared from the works of Ibn Katheer, At-Tabari, As-Syooti, and other historians.* El-Mansoura: Dar al-Manarah, 2001.

Kāmil, 'Abd al-'Azīz 'Abd al-Qādir. *Islam and the Race Question.* Paris: UNESCO, 1970.

Khadduri, Majid. *Al-Shafi'i's Risala.* Cambridge: The Islamic Texts Society, 2008.

Khan, Muḥammad Muhsin and Al-Hilālī, Muḥammad Taqi-ud-Din (trans.). *The Noble Qur'ān.* Riyadh: Darussalam, 2001.

Kilson, Martin. *The African Diaspora.* Massachusetts: Harvard University Press, 1976.

Kvam, Kristen, Schearing, Linda S. and Ziegler, Valarie H. *Eve & Adam.* Bloomington: Indiana University Press, 1999.

Lane, Edward William. *Arabic-English Lexicon: Volume 1 and 2.* Cambridge: The Islamic Texts Society, 1984.

Larsson, Gőran. *Ibn García's Shu'ūbiyya Letter: Ethnic and Theological Tensions in Medieval al-Andalus.* Leiden: Brill, 2003.

Lewis, Bernard. *Islam Volume I: Politics and War.* Oxford: Oxford University Press, 1974.

——. *Islam Volume II: Religion and Society.* Oxford: Oxford University Press, 1987.

Lewis, Bernard. "Race and Color in Islam." In *The African Diaspora: Interpretive Essays*, by M. L. Kilson and R. I. Rotberg, 37-56. 1976.

——. *Race and Slavery in the Middle East.* New York: Oxford University Press, 1990.

——. "The African Diaspora and the Civilisation of Islam." In *The African Diaspora*, by Martin Kilson, 48-49. Massachusetts: Harvard University Press, 1976.

——. *The Arabs in History.* Oxford: Oxford University Press, 1993.

——. *The Middle East: 200 Years of History from the Rise of Christianity to the Present Day.* London: Phoenix Press, 2000.

Lings, Martin. *Muḥammad: his life based on the earliest sources.* Vermont: Inner Traditions International, 1983.

Madani, Mohsen Saeidi, *Impact of Hindu Culture on Muslims.* New Delhi: M D Publications, 1993.

Mack, Beverly B. and Boyd, Jean. *One Woman's Jihad: Nana Asma'u, scholar and scribe.* Bloomington, IN: Indiana University Press, 2000.

Maknoon, Al-Ḥajj Mekaeel. *The Universal Significance of Adam.* London: Al-Meezaan Publications, 1998.

Marlow, Louise. *Hierarchy and Egalitarianism in Islamic Thought.* Cambridge: Cambridge University Press, 1997.

Mathers, E.P. *The Book of the Thousand and One Nights.* London: Routledge, 1990.

McEwan, P. J. M. (ed.). *Africa from Early Times to 1800.* Oxford: Oxford University Press, 1968.

Muḥammad, Akbar. "The Image of Africans in Arabic Literature: Some Unpublished Manuscripts." In *Slaves and Slavery in Muslim Africa, Volume 1: Islam and the Ideology of Enslavement*, by John Ralph Willis, 47-74. London: Frank Cass, 1985.

Muḥammad, Wesley. *Black Arabia & The African Origin of Islam.* [Place of publication unknown]: A-Team Publishing, 2009.

Mukhtar, al-Baqir al-'Afif. "The Crisis of Identity in Northern Sudan: A Dilemma of Black People with a White Culture." *Al-Khatim Adlan Centre for Enlightenment and Human Development.* http://www.kacesudan.org/files/x2yw43vg57.pdf (accessed 3 June 2009).

Myers, Walter Dean. *Malcolm X: By Any Means Necessary.* New York: Scholastic, 1993.

Ogot, Bethwell A. *Africa from the Sixteenth to the Eighteenth Century.* California: University of California Press, 1992.

Oluruntimeehim, B. O. *The Segu Tukulor Empire.* New York: Humanities Press, 1972.

Pellat, Charles (translated by D. M. Hawke). *The Life and Works of Jāḥiẓ.* California: University of California Press, 1969.

Pieterse, Jan Nederveen. *White on Black: Images of Africa and Blacks in Western Popular Culture.* London: Yale University Press, 1992.

Popovic, Alexandre. *The Revolt of African Slaves in Iraq.* Princeton: Markus Wiener Publishers, 1999.

Qadhi, Abu Ammaar Yasir. *An Introduction to the Sciences of the Qur'aan.* Birmingham: Al-Hidaayah, 1999.

Quick, Abdullah Hakim. *Deeper Roots: Muslims in the Americas and the Caribbean From Before Columbus To the Present.* London: Ta-Ha Publishers, 1998.

Qureshi, Sultan Ahmed. *Letters of the Holy Prophet.* Lahore: Muslim Educational Trust, [n.d.].

Reddie, Richard S. *Black Muslims in Britain.* Oxford: Lion, 2009.

Robinson, David. *Muslim Societies in African History.* New York: Cambridge University Press, 2004.

——. *The Holy War of Umar Tal.* Oxford: Oxford University Press, 1985.

Ruedy, John. *Modern Algeria: The Origins and Development of a Nation.* Bloomington: Indiana University Press, 1992.

Ryan, Patrick J. *Imale: Yoruba Participation in the Muslim Tradition.* Missoula, Montana: Scholars Press, 1978.

Segal, Ronald. *Islam's Black Slaves: A History of Africa's other Black Diaspora.* London: Atlantic Books, 2001.

——. *The Black Diaspora.* London: Faber and Faber, 1995.

Shakir, Zaid. "Islam, Prophet Muḥammad and Blackness." *Lampost Productions.* http://www.lamppostproductions.com/files/articles/The%20Prophet%20and%20Blackness.pdf (accessed May 26, 2009).

Sheik-Abdi, Abdi. *Divine Madness: Mohammed Abdulle Hassan of Somalia (1856-1920).* London: Zed Books, 1992.

Ṣihāb ad-Din, Ahmad bin 'Abd al-Qader bin Salem bin Utman (translated by Paul Lester Stenhouse). *Futuh al-Habasa: The Conquest of Abyssinia.* California: Tsehai Publishers, 2003.

Sotoodeh, M. (ed.) (translated by V. Minorsky). *Hudud al-'Alam: The Regions of the World.* E. J. W. Gibb Memorial, 1982.

Southgate, Minoo. "The negative images of blacks in some Medieval Iranian writings." *Iranian Studies, 17,* 1984: 3-36.

Sulaiman, Ibraheem. *The African Caliphate: The Life, Works and Teachings of Shaykh Usman dan Fodio.* London: Diwan Press, 2009.

Taylor, Susan C. *Brown Skin: Dr. Susan C. Taylor's prescription for flawless skin, hair, and nails.* New York: HarperCollins, 2008.

Toynbee, Arnold. *A Study of History.* Oxford: Oxford University Press, 1987.

Trimingham, John Spencer. *A History of Islam in West Africa.* London: Oxford University Press, 1962.

——. *Islam in East Africa.* London: Oxford University Press, 1964.

Trimingham, John Spencer. *Islam in West Africa.* London: Oxford University Press, 1959.

——. *The Influence of Islam upon Africa.* London: Longmans, 1968.

Turner, Brent. *Islam in the African American Experience.* Bloomington: Indiana University Press, 1997.

Von Denffer, Ahmad. *Ulum al-Qur'ān: An Introduction to the Sciences of the Qur'ān.* Leicester: The Islamic Foundation, 2007.

Walker, Robin. *When We Ruled.* Every Generation Media, 2005.

Wehr, Hans. *Arabic-English Dictionary.* New York: Spoken Language Services, 1976.

Williams, Chancellor. *The Destruction of Black Civilisation: Great Issues of Race from 4500 B.C. to 2000 A.D.* Chicago: Third World Press, 1987.

Willis, J. R. (ed.). *Slaves and Slavery in Muslim Africa (vol. 1): Islam and the Ideology of Slavery.* London: Frank Cass, 1985.

——. *Slaves and Slavery in Muslim Africa (vol. 2): The Service Estate.* London: Frank Cass, 1985.

X, Malcolm and Haley, Alex. *The Autobiography of Malcolm X.* London: Penguin Books, 1965.

X, Malcolm. *Malcolm X - February 1965: The Final Speeches/edited by Steve Clarke.* New York: Pathfinder, 2008.

——. *Malcolm X Speaks: selected speeches and statements/edited by George Breitman.* New York: Grove Press, 1990.

Yūsuf, Hamza and Shakir, Zaid. *Agenda to Change Our Condition.* California: Zaytuna Institute, 2008.

Index